Now What Shall We Do?

Now What

Shall We Do?

The Family Book
of Things to Do
and Games to Play

by

Emily R. Dow

illustrated by the author

Gramercy Publishing Company
New York

To all the boys and girls
who have asked me to write this book,
especially
Nicholas, Julia, Belinda, Daragh, Sioban, Clare,
Mike, Nancy, Brian, Melissa, Bim, True, Robert,
Peter, Winthrop, Jr., Katrina, and Nicole

Contents

FOREWORD ix

ONE THINGS TO DO ON SPECIAL DAYS 1
Valentine's Day • April Fool's Day • Easter
May Day • Mother's Day • Father's Day
Fourth of July • Election Day • Halloween
Thanksgiving • Christmas • Birthdays

TWO SUMMER ACTIVITIES 85
Games to play out of doors
Hobbies and things to make

THREE RAINY AND STAY-IN-BED DAYS 111
Things to make
Games to play indoors

FOUR HOLIDAY GREETING CARDS 153
When to send cards
How to make your own greeting cards

FIVE FAMILY GAMES • CAR GAMES
PARTY GAMES • GAMES TO PLAY ALONE 167

SIX PUZZLES AND GAMES TO PLAY ALONE 191
Scrambles • Mazes • Word games

SEVEN INDOOR WORK SHOP 207
Carpentry

EIGHT COSTUMES
FOR HOLIDAY PARADES AND PARTIES 227
Costume make-up
How to make the costumes

NINE WEATHER FORECASTING 247

Foreword

This is not a "do-it-yourself" book but rather a "doing-things-together" book.

Holidays, especially, are when families can be together more, when parents and children have time for hobbies, crafts, parties, and games. So this book follows the seasons and holidays, with all the family included.

But many of the crafts you can do alone. Someone sick in bed, or convalescing, often wants things to do that will require little or no help from the rest of the family. Then there are times in the year when one has a secret project, something to make as a surprise for another member of the family.

So this is a family book of doing things together and for each other all the year around.

Emily R. Dow

Now What Shall We Do?

Chapter 1

Things to Do on Special Days

Valentine's Day
April Fool's Day
Easter
May Day
Mother's Day
Father's Day
Fourth of July
Election Day
Halloween
Thanksgiving
Christmas
Birthdays

Three Valentine Presents
(To make for Grandparents, Aunts, or a sick friend)

A VALENTINE BOOK MARK

MATERIALS: A piece of red ribbon about an inch wide
and 12 inches long
Heavy white paper
Scissors
Paste
Crayons

CUT OUT six small white paper hearts—all the same size.

PASTE three of the hearts to the front of the ribbon, turn
it over, and paste the other three to the back of each
heart.

WRITE this message on the hearts—one word on each
heart: "I LOVE YOU."

A VALENTINE BLOTTER

MATERIALS: Three pieces of blotting paper about 6″
square (two of one color, and a third of
another color)

Scissors

Paste

A small picture—color one yourself or cut one from a magazine

CUT OUT three hearts from the blotting paper: a large and a small one of one color, and a middle-sized one of another color.

PASTE the three hearts together—with the largest on the bottom, the smallest on the top, and the middle-sized one in between.

PASTE the small picture on top of the three hearts.

A Valentine Pin Cushion

MATERIALS: Two pieces of red felt 4″ or 5″ square

Odd tiny pieces of colored felt and matching embroidery cotton

Cotton padding to stuff the pin cushion

A needle

Paper

Pencil

Scissors

(½ yard of narrow lace is optional—if you
want to trim the edge with it)

DRAW a heart pattern—small enough to fit the red felt
pieces.

CUT two hearts from the felt, using the pattern just made.

SEW small colored felt pieces to the front half of one
heart (placing them so they look like flowers and
leaves).

OVERCAST the two felt hearts together, using matching
or contrasting embroidery cotton, overcasting around the
edge.

LEAVE a small opening (about 1½″ wide) where you
can slide in the cotton stuffing.

FILL the valentine as full of cotton padding as you can
stuff it, then overcast the edge at the opening.

LACE may be sewed around the heart. To do this, rest
the bottom edge of the lace even with the overcast edge

of the heart, and overcast the two together. Make tiny pleats or gathers in the lace, as you sew it to the heart. This will make it look frilly when it is spread back.

A Valentine Party

THE INVITATION might be written on a valentine, but original valentine invitations are fun to make if you like to work with water color or poster paint. Here are a few suggestions:

CUT OUT two hearts, connected by a fold at the top or side. (See illustration.) Use red construction paper, decorate the card with white hearts and print the invitation with white ink; or use white paper, paint red hearts to decorate it, then print the invitation in red ink.

TABLE DECORATIONS should be red and white. Use a large white linen or paper table cloth and scatter red hearts of different sizes on it.

THE PLACE CARDS could be made from tiny valentines, or white cards decorated with red hearts.

A VALENTINE MOBILE hung over the center of the table, (from the ceiling or an over-head light) makes a colorful centerpiece.

MATERIALS: A large paper plate
Two larger paper doilies
Narrow red ribbon or red string
Paste
Assorted red and white hearts,
cupids, etc.

PASTE the paper doilies to the top and bottom of

the plate. Tie different lengths of red string through the rim of the plate—leaving a knot on the top side and the long end on the bottom. Paste or tie the hearts and cupids to the string ends.

TO HANG the mobile, tie four strings or ribbons, of equal length and equally spaced, to the top of the plate rim. Join the ends where they tie to the light.

REFRESHMENTS: Pimentos can be cut into tiny hearts to decorate open sandwiches and canapés. A tomato aspic salad might be moulded in a heart-shaped tin. A heart-shaped cake can be cut from a square or round cake (after it is baked and cool), by cutting around a paper heart pattern. Strawberry or raspberry jam make good coloring with white frosting.

GAMES should be planned to include valentines and hearts as much as possible. If the game calls for players in pairs, cut valentines in half—one for each two guests, and have the guests draw the pieces from a hat, then match the halves to find partners.

"FIND THE HEART" is a good writing game. Give each player a sheet of paper and pencil and ask him to write as many words as he can that have the five letters H-E-A-R-T in them. The letters do not have to be in sequence. They may be separated by any number of letters. For example: *H E A* D - *S T R O N G*.

ANOTHER WRITING GAME is to list all the words one can find in the name VALENTINE·

"TOSS THE HEARTS" is fun for any age group. Make six or eight hearts from cardboard—about the size of a playing card, and let each guest try to toss them into a hat. They should stand at a distance of three or four feet.

Some April Fool Tricks

GIVE A PIECE OF PAPER and pencil to someone. Ask him to write a message on the paper, toss it into the air, and then step on it. When he has done this, explain that you will tell him what is on that piece of paper. Of course he will say you can't. But—you tell him, "Your *foot* is! April Fool!"

THIS IS A GOOD TRICK to play on a grown up. You will need an electric light bulb for it. Ask someone to put his finger through the crack in a door—somewhere between the two hinges. Then give him a light bulb to hold there. When he is all set, holding the bulb, walk away and leave him. He will be helpless and unless someone comes to his assistance, he will have to drop the bulb. (Don't let him come to that, but tease him by calling, "April Fool," before you help him.)

Put Yourself Through a Piece of Paper

USE a piece of paper about 12″ by 15″—or half a page of newspaper. Show your audience the paper and tell them you can put yourself through it. Let them guess how, before you show them.

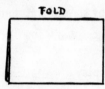

FOLD the paper in half the long way and lay it on the floor or on a table while you cut it.

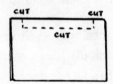

CUT OFF the folded edge, beginning an inch from each side, and making the cut about an inch deep. (See the illustration.)

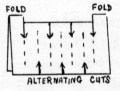

CUT straight lines in the paper about every inch, cutting through the two thicknesses. Make the cuts first from the fold side, then from the opposite side, cutting to about an inch of the edge—not all the way across. (See illustration.)

OPEN the cut paper, and carefully stretch it so that you can put it over your head and down over your body to your feet.

Jokes

HERE are some jokes to play on your friends. Ask them to do these things, and when they fail, show them how it is done.

KISS a box inside and outside, without taking off the cover.
(Kiss it indoors and outdoors.)

PUT one hand where the other hand cannot touch it.
(Put it on the elbow of the other arm.)

BITE an inch off a chair.
(Put the chair an inch away and bite.)

MAKE a pile of books as high as your head. Then take off your shoes and jump over them.
(Jump over the shoes.)

ASK me a question that I can only answer by saying, "Yes."
(What does Y-E-S spell?)

PUT a handerchief on the floor and have two people stand on it in such a way that they cannot touch one another.

(Put it on the doorsill and then shut the door between them.)

GO OUT of the room with two legs, and come back with six.

(Walk out of the room and come back carrying a chair.)

PUT yourself through a keyhole.

(Write the word, "Yourself," on a piece of paper, and put it through the keyhole.)

HAND someone an apple and a knife, telling him that if he can devide the fruit into four equal parts, you will give him a quarter.

(Of course he will cut it very carefully, into halves, and then quarters. When he has finished, ask him to hand you the pieces. Pretend to examine them carefully, after you have looked each piece over, give him a piece and say, "Here is your quarter.")

A Bunny Rabbit Hat for Easter

MATERIALS: Two sausage-shaped white balloons
                 White string

Heavy white cardboard 12″ by 13″

BLOW up the balloons and tie one to each end of the cardboard strip, about an inch from the edge. Have the string that ties it long enough to reach under your chin. Put the cardboard over your head, and tie it under the chin.

An Easter Egg Tree

MATERIALS: Five eggs
Vegetable coloring
Glue
Aluminum foil
Small beads and sequins
A crochet hook (or long darning needle)
String

Aluminum paint
A small branch (about 15″ tall)
A bowl of sand
Ten small flat buttons

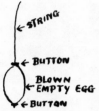

BLOW the egg from the shell of each of the five eggs. (Save this for scrambled eggs.) To blow an egg, pick a hole in the top and bottom ends. Blow into the top hole and the egg will come out the bottom. It takes a lot of hard blowing. The pricks can be fairly large because they will be covered up when the eggs are hung on the tree.

COLOR the blown eggs with vegetable dye, and decorate them by gluing on sequins and beads.

PAINT the branch with aluminum paint. After it is dry, stick it in a colored bowl filled with sand—or use crumpled foil to hold it straight.

HANG the colored Easter eggs on the branch by threading a string through each egg. Use the crochet hook or long needle for this, and fasten a button over the bottom hole to hold the string, then thread another button through the string to cover up the top hole.

MAKE some tiny birds and butterflies of the foil, if you like, and attach these to the branch too.

An Easter Corsage

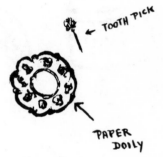

TOOTH PICK

PAPER DOILY

MATERIALS: Small paper doilies
Bits of colored tissue paper
Toothpicks
Paste
Aluminum foil
Scissors

CUT the colored tissue paper into small pieces. Fringe each piece and squeeze it into a tiny bit. Paste this to the top of the paper doily. Use a few green pieces among the other colors so when they are all pasted to the top of the doily, they will look like little flowers.

WRAP two of the colored bits of tissue paper to the tops of two toothpicks, and stick the other ends of the toothpicks through the doily, wrapping the underside with aluminum foil. (To make it look like wrapped flower stems.)

ALUMINUM FOIL OVER TOOTH PICKS

A CORSAGE BOX can be made from a small cylinder-shaped ice cream carton. Cover the carton with flowered wallpaper. Cut a piece of wallpaper the height of the box and paste it around the sides. Lay the top of the box on a piece of the paper and draw around it. Cut this out and paste it to the cover. Then paste a strip of the wallpaper around the sides of the cover. Make a small hole on each side of the box and run ribbons through— leaving a knot in the end of each ribbon on the inside. The ribbons can be tied in a bow across the cover. This will also serve as a handle.

May Baskets

MATERIALS: Heavy white paper
Colored tissue paper
Scissors
Paste

FIRST make a box or cornucopia from the heavy white paper. (Or perhaps you have a clean white box you would like to use instead of making one.)

A BOX is made by folding a piece of paper in half four times. Open the paper and you will find sixteen sections marked off by folds. Cut off four of these sections on one side. This gives you a strip which can be used for a handle on the May Basket. Now on the two shorter sides of the other piece of paper, cut along the center folds as far as the first cross fold. (See illustration.) Paste these three sections together on each side, by putting the paste on the corner sections and fastening them to the center one.

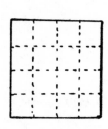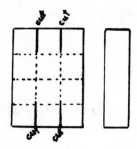

THE HANDLE should be pasted with the ends of the strip inside the middle of the two long sides of the box.

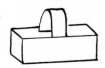

THE CORNUCOPIA is made by rolling a piece of paper into a cone. Use paste to hold it together, and fasten it so that the small end of the cone makes a point.

THE HANDLE for this May Basket is made from a long strip of paper, doubled over to form a loop, with the two ends pasted to the highest point of the top edge.

PAPER CURLS to trim the May Baskets can be made from colored tissue paper. Cut long strips of the paper—about an inch wide, and fringe one side by cutting lines ¼ inch apart and ⅝ of an inch deep. Lay this strip flat on a table, and holding the uncut edge, rub a table knife over the fringe. This must be done very carefully for the paper is easily torn. Paste these curls around the box—or cornucopia—by wrapping the strip around the bottom sides first, and adding one strip above another until the top is reached. Put the paste on the box, or cone, instead of on the tissue paper.

May Party Favors and Decorations

A MAY POLE CENTERPIECE can be made by nailing a round wooden stick to a heavy piece of cardboard. Have this pole about twelve inches high and be sure the cardboard is heavy enough to hold the stick upright. Wind the stick with narrow ribbon. Now on the top, tack one end of a ribbon for each guest and have each ribbon extend to the guest's place at the table. Tie a favor to this end of the ribbon.

FOR FAVORS give tiny dolls to the girls, and a small toy airplane to the boys. For older guests, make the Gum Drop Flowers described below.

GUM DROP FLOWERS: Take all the leaves and berries from a twig of Barberry, or similar bush, and stick gum drops on the thorns. Use an empty spool for a flower pot stand, covering it with aluminum foil. Stick the gum drop flower branch in the top hole of the spool.

A MAY BASKET FAVOR can be made by dipping the top of a marshmallow into boiling water, then quickly rubbing it in a dish of small cake-trim candies. (A saucer with a few candies works better than a deep dish, because the wet marshmallow will make the candies very sticky. A shallow dish can be refilled as the candies become wet.) Assorted colors look best. After the candies have dried on the top of the marshmallow, make a handle on it, using thin green wire. Stick the ends in the sides of the marshmallow, rounding the top.

A PARTY FAVOR: This is made from a lollypop which is trimmed with a tiny fan.

USE heavy figured gift-wrap paper, or wallpaper,

for the fan. Cut it into a half circle about five inches in diameter.

FOLD the paper circle in half, making a quarter circle. Open the paper and fold half the bottom edge on both sides up the to center fold. Then fold back the same straight edges so they are even with the side folds. See illustration. Next fold the two outside edges to the back, even with the center fold.

FOLD

FOLD   FOLD

FOLD   FOLD

FOLD BACK

← FAN
← LOLLY POP

OPEN the paper and you will have a tiny fan.

TIE the bottom of the fan to the end of the lollypop stick. Use a narrow ribbon to tie it and make a small bow on the front.

Mother's Day Presents
(The second Sunday in May)

A STRAW POCKET BOOK FOR MOTHER

MATERIALS: A plain edged straw table mat (the pliable type)

　　　Two colors of yarn
　　　A darning needle and a button with a metal
　　　　　shank and a bar to hold it in place
　　　(If you do not have this kind of button
　　　　　bar, you can use a small flat button and
　　　　　sew it to the inside of the pocket book
　　　　　to hold the shank.)

THE MAT is folded into three sections. A small one will
be the flap, and two of equal size will be the pocket.
(See illustration.)

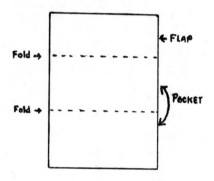

FOLD the bottom over the middle section—for the pocket,
and with one color yarn, overcast around all the edges
—except along the bottom fold. Do the same thing,
overcasting backward, with the other color yarn. This
will make a cross stitch border.

ON THE FLAP, in the middle of the edge, make a loop
of yarn and buttonhole stitch the loop. Fold down the
flap to find where the loop meets the pocket section, and

at that point attach the button to the outside of the pocket. Separate the straw to make a hole for inserting the shank, and fasten the metal bar to it on the inside— or sew the flat button to the inside.

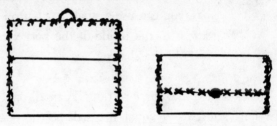

Oilcloth Table Mats

MATERIALS: Oilcloth of a plain color
      Scissors
      Oil paints
      A stiff paint brush (or tooth brush)
      Some heavy cardboard
      Candle wax (the end of an old candle.)

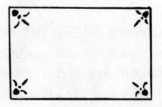

CUT the oilcloth into mats about 11″ by 15″

NOW cut a piece of cardboard the same size as the mats. On each corner of the cardboard, draw the design you would like to stencil on the oilcloth mats. A simple flower design, a star, or an animal might be used, but the figure should be divided into sections to make a good stencil. (See the illustration.)

WHEN you have drawn the stencil design, cut it out very carefully so the edges of the outline will be smooth.

NEXT melt the candle wax and pour it over the edges of the cut-out design. (A lighted candle held over it will drip a covering for the edges.) Be sure to have several layers of newspaper under the cardboard when you pour the candle wax.

WHEN the wax is dry, place the cardboard over the oilcloth mat and paint the cut-out design with oil paints.

FANCY PAPER NAPKINS

MATERIALS: Plain white paper napkins—any size you like
Water color paint

SPATTER and fold, the same way you would to make an

ink blot picture: Lay the open paper napkin on a news-paper and using any color water paint, spatter it over the napkin. Before the paint dries, carefully fold the napkin in half. Now open the napkin and spread it out to dry—paint side up—on a clean newspaper. If you want to use two colors, wait until one color dries before you spatter the napkin with a second color.

MAKE A BOX of fancy napkins of assorted colors, using this spatter method. They make nice birthday, Christmas, or Mother's Day presents.

Father's Day Presents
(The third Sunday in June)

A GLASS FOR TALL DRINKS

MAKE Dad his own tall glass for drinks and even plain iced tea or coffee will taste better in it.

MATERIALS: A plain tall glass—a jelly glass will do
Enamel or plastic paint
A paint brush or nail polish

IF you are clever with a paint brush, you can illustrate his favorite sport in the picture you paint on his glass. Look in the sporting magazines and see how to paint a duck, trout, or fishing lure, a deer, a golf bag and clubs, a sailboat, or a figure on skis.

PERHAPS you are not able to paint a picture on the glass, but you can still decorate it with fancy lettering. Use colored nail polish and print "For Dad" on the glass. Add a band of color or paint some dots on it too.

JEWEL TRIMMED BEVERAGE OPENER

MATERIALS: A beverage can opener
Water-proof cement
Sequins, spangles, rhinestones, glitter trim, etc.

SPREAD the handle of the metal opener with cement, and before it dries, add the glitter. (A pair of tweezers will help you sort out the small pieces.) This will make a very amusing Father's Day gift.

A MINK TRIMMED CAN OPENER

THIS makes another amusing gift for a man. If you have an odd piece of fur, cement this to the handle of the opener, cutting it to fit around the lid opener end.

Fourth of July Refreshments

A FIRECRACKER CUP, to hold nuts or candy, can be made from a toilet paper roll—or half a paper towel roll.

> CUT a circle of paper a little larger than the hole in the roll and fasten it over the end as you paste a band of red paper around the roll.

> FILL the red roll with nuts or candy, and push the end of a white string (about two inches long) into the middle of them, so it shows an inch above the top.

A ROUND CAKE, frosted to look like a drum, will add a patriotic touch to a Fourth of July party. It should be either a round layer cake, or an angel cake with cardboard placed over the hole before the cake is frosted.

> MAKE a white frosting and divide it into three bowls. Use vegetable coloring and make one bowl of frosting red, one blue, and leave the third white.

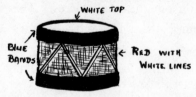

FROST the top of the cake with white, the sides with red. With the blue, make a band all around the top and bottom sides of the cake. When the frosting has hardened, make diagonal lines of white frosting all around the sides of the cake—from the top to the bottom blue bands. This is to represent the strings of the drum.

INDIVIDUAL CUP CAKE DRUMS are fun for children, but take more time and patience.

A TINY FLAG stuck in frosted cookies set in front of each place help to decorate the table.

Election Day Lapel Clips

MATERIALS: Pieces of gray and white felt
                Needle
                Thread
                Scissors
                A small paper clip

FOR THE ELEPHANT

CUT a triangle shape piece from the gray felt, making the

base 2½″ and the two sides 2″. Cut the white felt into two pieces ½″ by ⅛″, and make one end pointed.

ROLL UP the gray felt piece tightly, starting on one corner of the long side. Sew along the exposed edge to keep the roll together.

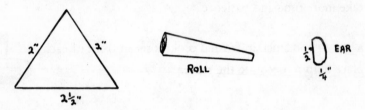

CUT OUT two ears. Make them ½″ long and ¼″ wide. Round the top and bottom, sew these to the head of the elephant (the large end of the roll).

EMBROIDER two eyes with black thread.

SEW the two white pieces on for tusks.

SEW a paper clip to the back of the head—fastening it at the single loop end.

FOR THE DONKEY

CUT a rectangle piece from the felt, making it 2½″ at the base, 2″ at the top, and 1″ on each side.

ROLL UP the felt piece tightly, starting on one corner of

the long edge. Sew the exposed edge down to hold the roll together.

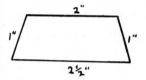

CUT OUT two ears. Make them 1″ long and ½″ wide. Round off the top of the ears and fold the ear in half at the bottom edge.

SEW the ears to the donkey's head along the doubled bottom edge. (The donkey's head is the large end of the roll.)

EMBROIDER two eyes and a mouth with black thread.

SEW a paper clip to the back of the head—fastening it at the single loop end.

A Halloween Mobile

MATERIALS: A straw
String
White paper
A straight pin

Pencil
Scissors

CUT two small ghosts from the white paper and draw their faces. Make them the same size but not the same shape.

TIE a piece of string around the middle of the straw and make a square knot to hold it. Now tie the two ends of the string together so there will be a loop.

SQUARE KNOT

PRICK a small hole in the top of each ghost head (with a pin). Cut two pieces of string, each one the same length, and thread one through each ghost. Tie a knot in the end of the string—on the back of the head—so that it will not pull out. Tie the other end of the string to the end of the straw.

HANG your mobile where the ghosts can move as the breeze blows them (a wall or ceiling light, or in a doorway).

Halloween Masks

MATERIALS: Heavy paper or lightweight cardboard
A pencil
Crayons
Scissors
Paste
A piece of fur (or cotton, wood shavings, or corn silk)
Sticky tape
Gummed reinforcements
An elastic
(You may not need all these things, but the more you have the more elaborate mask can be made.)

USING the heavy paper, cut a hole for your nose, then hold the paper up to your face and mark where the eyes and mouth should be.

THE FUR, cotton, or corn silk can be pasted to the mask

—to represent a mustache, eyebrows, etc. Corn silk is especially good for making hair.

STICKY TAPE can be used to attach a nose. Fold or roll a piece of paper and stick it on for the nose. (You might color the paper red first if you want the face to be ugly.)

FASTEN the piece of elastic to each side of the mask. Be sure it is long enough to reach across the back of your head when you wear the mask. Use the gummed reinforcements over the holes where the elastic is attached. This will prevent the mask from tearing.

Halloween Stunts and Party Games

BLINDFOLD each guest and give him a pencil and a piece of paper. Then ask him to draw a house—with windows, door, and a chimney. (You will have a collection of queer pictures.)

TWO PEOPLE are blindfolded and sit on the floor with a bowl of popcorn between them. Each one is given a spoon to feed the popcorn to the other.

SIT ON THE FLOOR and have a bowl of beans in front of you. Now see how many of the beans you can spoon into a pie plate balanced on your head.

BLINDFOLD two people and place a dish with a piece of cheese on it at a distant spot in the room (under a chair, on a table, or behind a door.) See which one can find the cheese first.

MATCH BOX STUNTS: This is very amusing to watch. Select two players. One is given the slide cover of a small match box. He slips this over the end of his nose, then the other player tries to take it off and slip it onto his own nose, without using hands. The first player helps as much as he can.

ORANGE STUNT: This is also very amusing to watch. Select two players. One is given an orange which he must hold under his chin (no hands). The other player tries to get the orange under his own chin, without using hands. The first player helps as much as he can.

OBJECTS IN THE DARK: The players all sit in a circle on the floor. All the lights are turned out and a tray of objects is passed around. The objects can be felt, but not seen, and each one has a turn to examine them. When the tray has been passed around the circle, it is taken from the room and the lights are turned on. Then each player tries to write a list of what he thought was on it. Here are objects that might be used:

Some kind of fruit
A piece of money
A lump of sugar
A tea bag

A toothpick
A feather
A wishbone
A walnut
A cake of soap
A nail
A key
A crochet hook

JACK O'LANTERN CONTEST

MATERIALS: A small pumpkin for each guest
(If you cannot find enough small pump-
kins use apples instead.)
A knife
A small spoon
A tiny candle
A paper plate
(One of each of the above to go with each
pumpkin.)

THE OBJECT is for each guest to cut and scoop out the
pumpkin, and make a funny face on it, so it can be used
for a jack o'lantern. The paper plate is to hold the
seeds, etc.

WHEN the jack o'lanterns are all finished, place them
in a row on a table or mantle. Light the candles, and then
have all the guests select the funniest. This may be
done by giving each pumpkin a number and having the

guests write their selections on pieces of paper, so the votes can be sorted and counted.

Pass the Ice

TWO LINES are formed by the players. At one end of each line is a bowl of six cubes of ice. At the other end of each line is an empty bowl.

THE OBJECT is to pass the cubes of ice, one at a time, down the line, and deposit them in the bowl that was empty. If a cube is dropped as it is being passed, it must be rescued by the player who dropped it, and no ice can be passed beyond him during the time he is picking it up. Each player on one side must handle all six cubes of ice.

Bean Race

EACH PLAYER is given a straw, and two lines are formed with an even number on each side.

AN EMPTY MILK BOTTLE is placed at the end of each line, behind the last player.

A CUP OF BEANS—one bean for each player in the line —is placed in front of the first player.

THE OBJECT is for each line to transfer the beans from the cup to the milk bottle, by drawing through the straw so the bean will stick to it. At a given signal the first player in each line starts with his straw. As soon as he has taken a bean from the cup and starts back to the end of the line, the next player starts. If a bean is dropped it must be picked up with the straw.

Nut Crack Night
(Halloween)

HALLOWEEN in England is also "Nut Crack Night." Here is something they do over there on that night:

PLACE two nuts in the fire, side by side. Give a name to each nut—the names of possible husbands or wives—and the nut that glows the most brightly will be the lucky one. If the fire makes the nut crack and fly apart, it is a bad sign, but if both nuts burst together, it is a very good sign. TRY this at your Halloween Party.

Halloween Safety Measures

PAPER COSTUMES can be dangerous. Select a cloth one if you can, but if you must wear one made of paper, keep away from flames—candles, fireplaces, etc., and do not carry around a lighted candle, even if it is in a lantern.

CLOTH COSTUMES should be light colored so they can be seen by the motorist. If you must wear a dark colored costume, make it more spooky and safer by sticking on spots of reflecting tape.

FIREPROOF YOUR COSTUME by dipping it in a solution of borax and boric acid: to 2 quarts of water add 2 ounces of boric acid and 4½ ounces of borax. Soak it completely, then let it dry.

CARRY A FLASHLIGHT, or a battery controlled lantern, when you go out on Halloween. If you want to take a lighted pumpkin, use a small flashlight instead of a candle to light it.

KEEP OUT OF THE ROAD AND WALK ON THE SIDEWALK.

HAVE FUN

Raisin Turkeys
(For Thanksgiving favors or place cards)

MATERIALS: Raisins
Cranberries
Marshmallows
Sugar cookies
Toothpicks

THE BODY of the turkey is a marshmallow.

THE FEET are toothpick halves, and these are stuck into a sugar cookie to hold the turkey in a standing position.

THE NECK is a toothpick with raisins slipped on it.

THE HEAD is made of more raisins stuck together with bits of toothpick. The comb of the turkey is made of a piece of red cranberry.

THE TAIL has toothpicks filled with raisins, and grouped together to form a fan. The ends of these toothpicks are stuck into the back of the marshmallow body.

FASTEN the marshmallow body and toothpick feet to the cookie first, and then make the turkey's neck and head. The tail should be made last, for each toothpick has to be stuck into the marshmallow carefully so the turkey will balance and not tip over.

A Turkey Place Card

MATERIALS: Small white cards 2″ by 2½″
Tiny pine cones ¾″ to 1″ long
Brown, yellow, and red construction paper
Glue

CUT the pieces as illustrated.

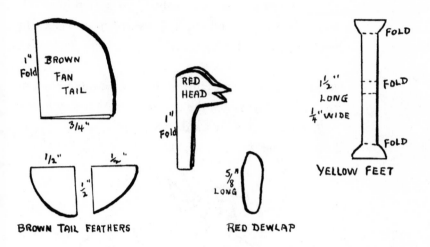

COVER the inside of the head piece with glue and slip the bottom of the neck under a scale on the front of the stem end of a small pine cone.

SLIP the edge of the dewlap between the neck pieces and squeeze the neck and the top of the head piece together.

COLOR a black dot eye on both sides of the head.

COVER the inside bottom straight edge of the fan tail with glue, on both sides of the fold, and slip this over some of the scales at the other end of the cone.

GLUE the two tail feathers to both sides of the cone, slipping the pointed end under a scale, where it will protrude at the lower back of the turkey.

MAKE two folds in the middle of the foot piece, dividing it into three sections. Cover both sides of this middle section with glue and slip it between the scales at the bottom of the turkey.

FOLD the feet up and put a little glue on the bottom of each foot. Now fasten the two feet of the turkey to one corner of a small white card.

A Tarlatan Christmas Tree

MATERIALS: One yard green tarlatan
A white candle
A candle holder
Scissors (if you have pinking shears, use them)
A small box of colored stars

FIRST draw a star on paper. Make it a many pointed star —like the illustration. (This star may be used for a pattern. Trace around it, using a piece of tissue paper.)

USE this pattern for your top star. Pin the paper pattern to your tarlatan cloth and cut a tarlatan star—using pinking shears if you have them.

NOW lay the tarlatan star you have just cut on another piece of tarlatan and cut a little larger star (about ¼ inch larger.) Cut as many stars as you want this same way. Make each star a little larger than the one before. You should have at least fifteen stars for a short candle and more if the candle is tall.

NEXT paste small colored stars to the tarlatan stars.

NOW beginning with the largest star you cut, make a small crosscut in the center and slip it over the candle. Slide it down to the bottom just above the holder. Then take the next largest star and do the same—this time slipping it down the candle and leaving it just above the last star. Put all the tarlatan stars on the candle this way, until you have the smallest star at the top.

A Table Decoration
(For Christmas)

MATERIALS: A small aluminum foil pie plate (the kind
sold with frozen pies)
A red candle about eight inches tall
A few winter greens—twigs of pine
or hemlock.
Some small pine cones and red berries or
bittersweet
(If you live in the country, you will probably find some of these in your own yard)

MELT the bottom end of the candle enough to make it
stick and stand in the center of the pie plate. One way
to do this is to heat the plate on the top of a radiator.
When the plate is hot, hold the candle in place until it
melts enough to stick.

ARRANGE the greens and cones around the candle in the
dish. Then scatter some of the bittersweet or red berries
here and there among the greens.

Christmas Candles

MATERIALS: Odds and ends of candles the same color
One whole candle, taller than you wish to
make your candle

> Two poultry pins or long corsage pins
> One milk or ice cream carton—with
> straight sides and broad base
> Two or more cakes paraffin
> A double boiler
> An egg beater
> A spatula
> An aluminum or tin pie plate
> Sparkles or sequins

TRY a small candle first and do not be in a hurry with it.

MELT the odd candles in a double boiler. Remove the wicks with a fork or long stick. Add one cake of paraffin and let that melt. (The wax will not harm the cooking utensils you use.)

SET the carton in a pie plate and pour in enough melted wax to just cover the inside bottom of the carton.

STICK your whole candle in the wax at the exact center of the carton. Hold it in place until the wax hardens enough to keep it steady.

FASTEN the two pins to opposite sides of the candle, either resting them on the top edges of the carton (if the candle is taller than the box), or pricking through the sides. Stick the point of each pin into the candle to steady it and hold it in place. (See illustration.)

POUR wax into the carton, a little at a time, and let it set between each ¼ inch of added wax. Do not try to hurry or your middle candle will melt and ruin the final effect. Make the candle as tall as you like, but do not fill the carton to the top. Be sure the central candle stays in place. If you can carry it to the refrigerator without moving the pins that hold the middle candle, the wax will harden quicker between each pouring. After the last wax has been added, let it stand over night to be sure it has really hardened in the carton.

TEAR OFF the carton after the wax has hardened completely. You may find you have a hole at the top of the candle you made. If so, add a little more wax to cover it. If the center candle sticks up in the middle, light it and let it burn down to the level of the other wax. Add a little wax of the right color to cover the center.

To Trim the Candle

MELT a cake of paraffin in a double boiler. Take it from the heat.

FROSTED CANDLE

WHIP the melted wax with an egg beater. It takes a long time—longer than whipping eggs. When it looks like stiffly beaten egg whites, frost your candle with it. Use the spatula and work quickly. Rough it up and down, around the candle, and in a pattern. Have it frosted thin enough so the color shows through.

BEFORE it hardens, sprinkle it with sparkles or sequins.

Two people should work together on a candle because the wax hardens quickly and the sparkles should be put on while the foamy wax is being spread on the candle.

A Christmas Angel

MATERIALS: Gold wrapping paper
Silver paper or aluminum foil
A pipe cleaner
Christmas tree tinsel
Light weight cardboard
Glue
Scissors

FOR THE HEAD of the angel, there are many possibilities: a ping pong ball, a large wooden bead, the round plastic box sold with a dress zipper, a small empty spool, or two white medicine bottle caps glued together.

TO MAKE THE FACE you will need crayons, paint, or nail polish. A face can be drawn on the ping pong ball and the white bottle cap, but if you use a spool or zipper box for a head, you will need to cut a round piece of white paper to glue to the front for the face. Paint the face before you glue the doll together.

MAKE A STAND for the doll by cutting a half circle from

cardboard. Roll this into a cone shape and glue or staple it together. When it is dry, cover the stand with silver paper.

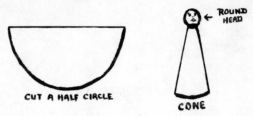

CUT A HALF CIRCLE   CONE

CUT another half circle from the gold paper. Make this larger than the cardboard circle and roll it over the silver cone to make the angel's robe. Glue it in place.

GLUE the head to the top of the cone. Around the back of the head, glue circular rows of Christmas tree tinsel. Make a double row at the top for a halo.

WIND a pipe cleaner with a narrow strip of silver paper. Slip the cleaner through the doll's robe by making a small hole at each side where the arms should come. Cross the two ends in front.

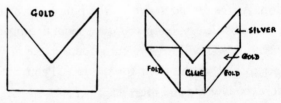

CUT angel wings from the gold paper. (See illustration.) Cover the back side of the wings with silver paper. If the bottom edge of the wings are cut straight and the two lower points of the paper are folded up to the center, the wings will be more attractive as they will show both gold and silver from the front.

GLUE the wings to the back of the angel doll.

FOR A FIREPLACE MANTELPIECE make two or three Christmas angels. Cut and fold a small piece of gold or silver paper to make a book for each doll to hold, instead of crossing the pipe cleaner arms.

Christmas Tree Balls

MATERIALS: Eggs
Gold and silver paint or Easter egg dye
Glitter and artificial snow
Buttons

Red or green thread (preferably nylon)
A large thin darning needle
Glue

BLOW the eggs, the same way you do at Easter: by pricking a hole in the top and bottom and blowing the white and yolk from the egg.

COLOR the egg, either with Easter egg dye or gold and silver paint.

TRIM the egg with glitter or artificial snow. Apply the glue to the part you want trimmed and sprinkle the glitter over it.

SEW a red or green thread (double thickness) through the holes in the egg. Attach a button outside each hole, to hold the thread. Leave a loop three or four inches long at the top to hang the egg to the Christmas tree.

BEADS can be used instead of buttons, to hold the thread. A short string of several beads add to the ornament.

A Golden Bird's Nest

SAVE the bird's nest you pick up in the fall. It can be used for a Christmas decoration. Spray it with gold paint, and put tiny colored Christmas balls in it for eggs.

Christmas Tree Lantern

MATERIALS: Fancy paper
Scissors
Paste

THESE lanterns can be made from any color or grade of paper, but the fancier the paper, the more attractive the lantern will be. Heavy gilt or silver printed Christmas wrapping paper can be made into lovely tree ornament lanterns.

CUT the lantern from a small piece of folded paper. Six inches, by four inches is a good size. Large lanterns look out of place on a Christmas tree.

FOLD the paper in half the long way and cut slits from the folded edge to about ½ inch from the opposite edge. Have the slits spaced evenly—about ½ inch apart.

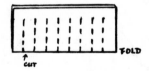

OPEN the paper and paste the two ends together.

CUT a narrow handle from the same color paper, making it ½ inch wide and about six inches long.

PASTE the handle to the top of the lantern, with the two

ends inside and the same distance apart on both sides so the lantern will hang straight.

WHEN you hang it on the Christmas tree, push up the middle folds to make the lantern spread in the middle.

A Bead Star for the Christmas Tree

MATERIALS: Three tiny invisible wire hair pins
Odd colored beads
A short piece of string

STRAIGHTEN each hair pin wire, then twist all three together at the centers, winding one over the other until they form a star shape, with all six points an equal distance apart. (See illustration.)

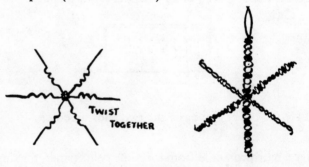

TWIST
TOGETHER

SLIP your colored beads over each wire point, filling it from the center to within about ⅛ inch from the end.

BEND over the end of each wire, after it has been filled with beads. This will hold them on the wire.

TIE a short string to one of the points so your star may be hung on the Christmas tree.

Christmas Decorations

BALL OF GREENS

MATERIALS: Strong red string
An orange
Silver or gold paint
Sprigs of hemlock, holly, or any greens you
want

TIE the red string around an orange two ways. Make a loop at the top so you can hang it up.

STICK greens into the orange until it is completely covered.

PAINT the ends of the greens with gold or silver paint.

HANG the orange ball in a doorway, from an overhead light, or from a fireplace mantel.

A Small Christmas Wreath

MATERIALS:　A jar rubber
Small wire hair pins, or thin wire
Narrow red ribbon
A tiny bell
A few greens—holly or pine

JAR RUBBER

WIRE the greens to the ring, using the hair pins. Tie a bow at the top of the wreath, and attach the bell to the bow.

HANG this small wreath in a window or over the mantel.

A Christmas Mobile

MATERIALS:　Heavy Christmas wrapping paper
Red or green string
A large button
Small tree ornaments
Paste
Scissors

CUT a half circle from the paper (use something round to draw your pattern—a dish, tray, etc.). Roll and paste the paper into a cone shape.

THREAD a piece of string through a button and with the button on the inside of the cone, pull the end of the string through the point of the cone. This string is to hang up the mobile.

PRICK holes around the edge of the cone and thread a string through each hole. Tie a knot on the inside end of the string, and fasten a small Christmas ornament to the other end. Have all the strings different lengths so the ornaments will not hang together.

HANG the mobile in a doorway, on a ceiling light, or over the stairs.

IF you prefer, you can make your own ornaments to hang from the mobile. Cut silhouettes of objects from colored paper.

A Christmas Apron

A CHRISTMAS apron can be part of the holiday decoration in the house. Make one for yourself. It also makes a nice gift for your hostess at a Christmas party.

RIBBON

MATERIALS: ½ yard tarlatan—either red or green

1½ yards ribbon the same color and 2" wide

Thread to match

8 tiny bells

2¼ yards narrow ribbon—red or green but not the same color as the tarlatan

FOLD the tarlatan in half—with the two finished edges together. Cut off the finished edges, and cut through the fold of the material so you have two layers of tarlatan with cut edges on all sides.

SEW along the double top edge and pull up the threads so the material is gathered to twelve inches.

FASTEN the two-inch ribbon to the gathered top. First pin the middle of the ribbon to the middle of the top. Even out the gathers and pin them to the edge of the ribbon. Sew one edge of the ribbon to the cloth, then turn the ribbon over the top of the gathered cloth and sew down the other edge of the ribbon.

CUT the narrow ribbon into eight pieces and make eight tiny bows from it.

SEW each bow, with a tiny bell attached, to the front of the apron.

CHRISTMAS FANS

MATERIALS: Heavy gold or silver paper
Glue
Scissors
Sequins
A piece of cardboard 3″ by 1″

CUT the paper any size you want but make it wider than it is tall. The height of your finished fan will be about one inch shorter than the height of the paper you use.

FOLD over the right edge of the paper, first to the front and then to the back. Continue doing this until you have pleated the entire piece of paper and made a long folded strip. Then with the paper still folded, turn up the bottom edge about one inch.

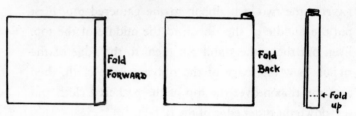

CUT a strip of matching paper two inches by three inches, and folding it in half the long way, glue this to the front and back of your piece of cardboard.

GLUE the turned up end of the fan to the middle of the covered cardboard and spread the folds of the fan so it opens as much as possible.

TRIM the fan by gluing sequins to it. This makes a pretty background for your Christmas angels and looks nice on a table or mantelpiece.

A Yarn Bouquet

This will make a nice Christmas present for a Grandmother or the Aunt who has everything.

MATERIALS: Pieces of colored yarn (some should be
green)
A table knife
Scissors

LAY a strip of green yarn the length of the knife blade,
then wind more yarn—of another color—over it and
around the blade. (You will need at least ten winds.)

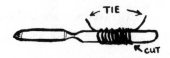

TIE together the two ends of green yarn. Make a strong
knot to hold all the threads tight.

NEXT cut the threads at the bottom edge of the knife.

MAKE several of these pompons of different colors. Tie
the stems together and you will have a pretty bunch of
yarn flowers.

FLOWERS TO WEAR ON A COAT LAPEL

MATERIALS: Bits of bright colored felt
Green yarn
An embroidery needle
Scissors

CUT pieces of felt to look like flower petals, or in the
shape of stars, or diamonds.

USING an embroidery needle and green yarn, sew one stitch through the center of each flower. (Put the needle through from the back and come out again on the same side.)

CUT OFF the yarn to leave two ends about two inches long—for flower stems. Tie these ends together under the flower petal.

MAKE several of these flowers and tie all the green stems together to make a flower corsage.

A DINAH DOORSTOP DOLL

MATERIALS: A bottle with a cork or small screw top (It should be about 10″ tall and 4″ wide at the bottom)
Some sand
A black sock
A piece of string
A needle and thread
Scissors
Crayons
¼ yard of dark blue or black cotton cloth
An 8″ square of red cotton cloth, and an 8″ square of bright blue cloth

Sawdust, shavings, or cotton—enough to
fill the toe of the sock

FIRST fill your bottle half full of sand, and put the top on.

CUT the foot of the sock in half and fill the toe end with
the cotton or sawdust.

SLIP the open end of the toe over the top of the bottle
and tie a string around the neck of the bottle to hold it
there.

THREAD your needle and, using a double thread with a
knot in the end, sew a running stitch across one long
side of the dark material.

PULL UP the stitches—to gather the cloth—and fasten it
around the bottle at the place where the sock is tied with
the string.

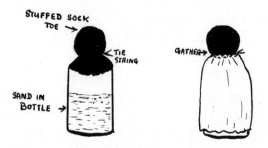

FOLD the blue eight-inch square of material diagonally,
and wrap it around the top of the bottle, just below the

sock head. (To make it look like a shawl.) Pin or sew it in place.

FOLD the red eight-inch square of material diagonally, and wrap that around the stuffed sock head—like a kerchief. Tie the ends and pin or sew them in place.

CRAYON some eyes, a nose and a mouth on the sock head.

THE DOLL is now ready to stand against the door to keep it open.

Christmas Presents to Make

A BUD VASE can be made from the plastic or glass tube that comes with a toothbrush. Use modeling clay to make a stand for it. Paint the stand with a bright enamel paint and decorate the top of the vase with a design or a band of the same color.

A DOLL for baby can be made from old spools. You will need three large and twelve small spools as well as four shoe strings. Tie the shoe strings together at one end and string them through a large spool (for the head.) Separate the strings and add three spools to two of them (for arms.) Tie a knot in each end. Now put the other two strings through two large spools for the body. At the bottom, separate the strings and add three small spools for the two legs. Tie a knot in each end. The top spool should have a face painted on it. You can use water color paints or nail polish.

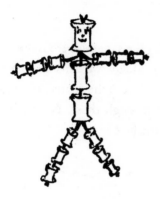

A GLASS PAPER WEIGHT makes a very nice gift for a relative if it has your own picture on it. Buy a paper weight that has a picture and felt pasted to the back and steam off the felt by holding it over the spout of a boiling tea kettle. Then remove the picture. Paste a snapshot of yourself on the back of the glass (face down.) Glue the felt to the back of the picture. Now turn the paperweight over and see how the glass improves the picture.

PINE CONE MATCH HOLDERS make good Christmas presents. Use the largest cones you can find. Cut off the stem end, making a flat surface so it will stand upright. Now paint the ends of the petals a bright color. When the paint is dry, put matches between the petals.

MAKE A CHRISTMAS NECKTIE for Dad or brother. You will need a bow-tie clip and a piece of red felt four inches by five inches. Also two or three green balls from ball fringe, or enough green yarn to make small pompon balls.

CUT two ties the same size from the red felt. (See illustration.) Make two slits in one tie—each one about ½ inch from the center, and slip the top ends of the clip through these. Now glue the other tie piece over the first.

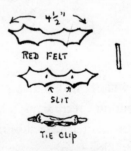

SEW a narrow strip of felt over the middle of the tie and the middle of the clip at the back.

GLUE the green pompon balls to the front of the tie, in the middle.

TO MAKE A SMALL POMPON: Wind yarn over a strip

of ½ inch wide cardboard (about twenty winds),
thread a doubled thread of the yarn through the
winds and tie the yarn tight. Now cut the yarn from
the cardboard opposite the tied ends.

SNOWMAN LAPEL ORNAMENT

MATERIALS: White yarn
Red, black, and white thread
A small piece of black felt
6″ of narrow red ribbon
A needle
Scissors

CUT the yarn to make the following lengths:
Twelve strands 6″ long
Six strands 5″ long

FOLD six of the long strands in half and wind red thread
tightly around them, about ½ inch from the folded end.
Do the same with the other six long strands.

FOLD in both ends of the short strands of yarn, so they
meet in the center. (See illustration.) Tie red thread
around the two folded ends as you did with the longer
strands of yarn.

PLACE the smaller tied strands across the middle of one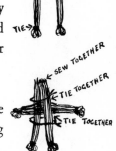
of the longer tied strands, then place the other long
strands on top of the two. (See illustration.)

TIE white yarn around the two long strands, just above and just below the center small strands.

WITH white thread, sew the loose top ends of yarn together so they may slip under the snowman's hat.

SEW black thread eyes, and a red thread mouth.

TIE the red ribbon around the snowman's neck, for a scarf.

TO MAKE THE HAT, cut the black felt into the following pieces:

Cut a circle ⅝ inch wide.

From the center of this circle, cut a small circle ¼ inch wide. (See illustration.) This is the hat brim. Cut a crown piece like the illustration, with the bottom edge 1 inch long and ¼ inch wide, and cut it with a ¼ inch circle attached to the center of the top edge.

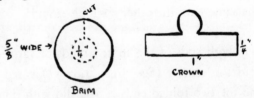

SEW the two ends of the crown together and fasten the round top piece down. Then sew the top of the hat to the circular brim.

NOW fasten the hat to the snowman's head.

A Christmas Gift Match Box

MATERIALS: Four small match boxes
Cardboard
Glue
Plastic paint
Trimmings: small sea shells, beads, sequins, or tiny pine cones may be used.

ARRANGE the match boxes in the order illustrated. First remove the matches. (Save them as you will want to refill the boxes when your gift is done.)

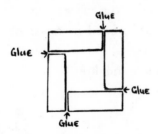

GLUE the box ends that touch one another.

CUT two pieces of cardboard the size and shape of the group and glue one to the top and the other to the bottom of the group.

PAINT the top, bottom and sides of the box. Leave the rough match-scratching surface unpainted, but paint the ends of the drawers.

GLUE a small shell or bead to each drawer for a handle.

DECORATE the top of the box—paint a design on it. Then glue a group of shells in the middle of the top, add beads, sequins or pine cones.

A CHRISTMAS HOBBY HORSE

MATERIALS: An old broom (or mop) handle
Red and green yarn
Red and green felt
A large (man-size) sock of white, black, or brown
Two black buttons the size of a dime
A roll of cotton wadding
1 yard of red or green ribbon about 1″ wide
Needle and thread
Scissors

STUFF the sock with enough cotton to make it stiff. Before filling the leg part of the sock, slip one end of the broom stick into the sock and stuff more cotton around it.

Gather up the edge of the sock with a needle and thread, fastening the gathers so the sock fits tight around the stick.

FROM FELT, cut out the following pieces in the shapes illustrated:

Two black ears—about four inches high, narrow at the top, and three inches wide at the bottom. With each piece of felt folded in half lengthwise, sew the doubled bottom edge of the ear to the side of the sock heel.

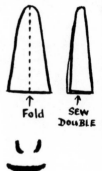

Three pieces of red felt for the nose and mouth. Sew these to the toe of the sock.

The harness may be made of either red or green felt. Measure your horse's head and cut the following strips ½ inch wide: one to go around the horse's head in front of the ears—the two ends sewed together; one to go around the end of the sock just above the horse's nose; and a third strip which goes across the back of the head, just behind the ears, with the two ends fastened to the corners of the mouth. Also fasten this band to the other two where it crosses them on each side of the head. (See illustration.)

RED AND GREEN YARN is used for the horse's mane. Use a large darning needle and sew long loops of yarn, straight down the horse's head, from between the ears to the stick.

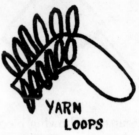

YARN
LOOPS

THE BLACK BUTTONS are sewed to the hobby horse for eyes.

A BRASS RING should be sewed to each corner of the red mouth—over the end of the felt harness.

FASTEN the ends of the ribbon to the two brass rings, to make reins.

Things to Sew for Christmas

A Travelling Shoe Bag

MATERIALS: A plastic vegetable bag (save the one food comes in at the market)

Cotton cloth a little larger than the bag (doubled)

A needle
Heavy embroidery or crochet cotton
A piece of twine or heavy string

FOLD the cotton cloth in half, with the wrong side out. Lay the plastic bag on the folded cloth, with one long side of the bag along the fold of the cloth.

CUT the cloth around the other three sides, about ½ inch from the edge of the plastic bag.

SEW along the bottom and the open side of the cloth bag you have just cut. (Be sure to sew it on the wrong side.) Turn the cotton bag right-side-out and put the plastic bag inside. Turn the outside edge at the open top inside, between the cloth and the plastic lining. Now overcast these two edges together, using the colored embroidery cotton.

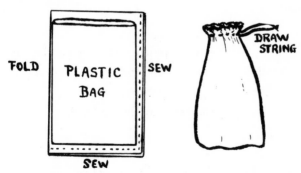

FOR A DRAW STRING, use the large needle and the heavy string or twine, and sew around the top edge of the bag. Leave long ends and tie them together with a double knot.

A Glasses Case for Christmas

MATERIALS: Two pieces of felt—larger than a pair of
            glasses
            A small piece of green felt
            Yarn in two colors, or embroidery silk
            A needle
            Scissors
            Some green thread
            A common pin
            Some colored sequins or beads

CUT the two felt pieces so they are 3″ wide, and 6½″
long. Round off the bottom corners. Cut a Christmas tree
from the green felt and pin it to the middle of one of
the large pieces of felt. Now sew sequins to the Christmas tree—to look like trimmings. Take out the pin
when the tree is thoroughly fastened down with the
sequins.

PUT the two felt pieces together and overcast the long
edges and the bottom—first one way with one color yarn,
and the other way with the other color yarn. (This will
make the two threads cross around the edge of the glasses
case.)

A Fancy Christmas Stocking

MATERIALS: Red and green felt, each piece measuring
            about 8″ by 10″

Smaller pieces of felt in other bright colors
Colored embroidery cotton
A few sequins or beads
A pair of pinking shears
A needle and scissors

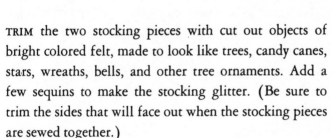

CUT a large stocking from the red felt—using pinking shears so the edge will be fancy. Cut another stocking from the green felt and make this about ¼ inch smaller all the way around. Cut this with the pinking shears too.

TRIM the two stocking pieces with cut out objects of bright colored felt, made to look like trees, candy canes, stars, wreaths, bells, and other tree ornaments. Add a few sequins to make the stocking glitter. (Be sure to trim the sides that will face out when the stocking pieces are sewed together.)

SEW the two pieces together with embroidery cotton. Use a bright color so the stitches will help trim the stocking. Sew up both sides and around the foot, but leave the top open.

CUT a small strip of green felt, about four inches long and ½ inch wide, and sew this in a loop to the top of the back seam of the stocking.

TABLE MAT CASE

MATERIALS: Four sheets of cardboard 15″ by 20″

1-1/3 yards chintz
Two yards 1" wide ribbon to match chintz

CUT the chintz to make four pieces 18" by 23".

COVER each of the four sheets of cardboard with the chintz. Fold it over the two long edges first and stick it in place with adhesive tape, then smooth it over the other two sides the same way.

BACK OF COVER

FASTEN each pair of covered pieces together (right sides out) by sewing the edges together. This can be done on a machine with a large needle and wide stitches, or it can be sewed by hand.

TIE the ribbon around the two covers, making a large bow so the ends will be long enough to reach around when the case is filled with table mats.

A Circus Party

THE INVITATION

ILLUSTRATE it with the picture of an animal. Cut a picture from a magazine, if you cannot draw your own, or use animal stickers.

The Games

ANIMAL GUESTS: As each guest arrives, pin the name of an animal on his back, and tell him he must guess who he is. The others may give him hints as they try to find out their own animal names.

TALKING ANIMALS: All the players sit in a circle. One person is chosen to be the animal trainer. He stands in the center, holds a stick in his hand, and walks around the circle slowly. Suddenly he stops and points his stick at someone, as he says, "Speak ....", and gives the name of a circus animal. The person to whom he points must make a noise like the animal named, before the trainer counts to ten. If he fails to respond, he must take the trainer's place.

HOW MANY ANIMALS: Give each guest a piece of paper and a pencil, and tell him to write the word ELE-PHANT. Then, at a given signal, the players are asked to write all the words they can make from the eight letters in that name.

AN ANIMAL OBSTACLE RACE: (To be played out doors.) The players must crawl on hands and knees, or "walk on all fours."

THE OBSTACLES: Crawl through a tent, or a blanket hung over a line and chairs. Drink a saucer of water, like an animal. (Have a saucer for each player.) Pick up these articles without using hands, and pile them at a specified place: a small ball, a piece of paper, a cookie, a stick, a shoe, a spoon, and a spool.

THE CAKE

THE REFRESHMENTS: Animal crackers can be used for cake and table decorations. The favors might be miniature animals. The ice cream should be served in cones, and the other food should be things one finds at a circus: hot dogs, pop corn, peanuts, and candy kisses.

A Balloon Party

INVITATIONS

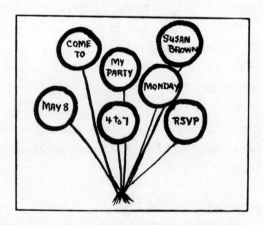

ON A WHITE CARD draw a bunch of balloons and paint

each one a different color. Write the invitation on the colored balloons.

The Games

GAMES TO PLAY at the party should include balloons as much as possible. Here are a few:

BALLOON RACE: Each player is given a deflated balloon. At a given signal (on the starting line), he must blow it up and run with it, full of air, to the other side of the race course. There he lets the air out. (He must slap it between his palms to prove it.) Then he blows it up again and runs back to the starting line with the balloon full of air.

The next in line does the same, but he cannot start to blow up his balloon until the first player touches him.

If the player accidently lets the air out of the balloon as he races from the start to the return, he must run back and start all over again.

The balloons must be blown to a fair size—bigger than a grapefruit, and there must be a balloon for each individual player. They are not to be passed from one to another.

ANOTHER BALLOON RACE: The players all stand in line. Each player is given a deflated balloon. At the first given signal he must blow up the balloon. Then at the next signal of, "Let it go", he stops blowing and tosses the balloon in front of him, to see how far it will go.

BALLOON ON A PLATE: This is another race. Each player is given a paper plate, and a balloon blown to a good size.

The players all start on a line. Each one must hold his left hand behind his back. In his right hand he has the plate with the balloon on it. This is the way he must race. At a signal, the players race to a given goal, carrying their balloons on the plates. They cannot touch the balloons with their left hands (which are held behind them), and if a balloon blows off, it must be picked up with the plate.

PASS THE BALLOON: All the players sit in a circle around the leader. An inflated balloon is passed around the circle, from one person to the next. When the leader calls, "Balloon", the player who is holding it must jump to his feet and recite a nursery rhyme as he tosses the balloon to the leader. If he is slow and does not finish the rhyme before the leader catches the balloon, he is out of the game. He may, however, toss the balloon so the leader has to jump around for it. But tossing it outside the circle puts him out of the game.

DECORATIONS

TIE an inflated balloon to each guest's chair at the table, and have his name on the balloon. Red nail polish can be used to write the name. For a centerpiece, tie a bunch of balloons to a heavy glass or metal flower holder (the flat kind with holes in it), and set the holder in a large bowl.

A *Mother Goose Party*
(For pre-school age children)

BEFORE you give this party, be sure to have a good, well-illustrated copy of *Mother Goose*, preferably with the rhymes set to music.

THE INVITATION

THIS might suggest that the children come dressed as Mother Goose characters.

THE GAMES

PIN THE MOUSE ON THE CLOCK: Have a large clock face drawn, and make the hands point to one o'clock. Let the children take turns (blindfolded), pinning on a tiny mouse cut from black paper. Be sure to show the children where the hands are pointing and tell them that the clock is striking "One" so the mouse should be pinned there.

JACK BE NIMBLE: Little children will enjoy taking turns

jumping over a small candlestick, while the rest of the
group repeats the rhyme:

> "Jack be nimble,
> Jack be quick,
> Jack jump over
> The candlestick."

A TOMMY TUCKER SING: Repeat the rhyme to the children, and suggest they all sing before their supper. If
you have a piano, accompany the singing:

> "Little Tommy Tucker
> Sings for his supper.
> What shall he eat?
> White bread and butter."

THE TABLE DECORATIONS

HAVE a Jack Horner Pie in the center of the table. Use a
large shallow bowl for it, and make a top crust of brown
wrapping paper. Cut out a few blackbirds from heavy
black paper—make only one or two large birds, or several tiny ones. Place these on top of the pie.

AT EACH PLACE have a lollypop king. Make this by standing the lollypop in a marshmallow. Draw and cut out a
face to paste on the front of the lollypop. Make a gold
paper crown for the head, and a red paper cape with a

white paper ruffle at the neck to cover the lollypop stick.

AFTER the children are seated at the table, sing, or repeat the rhyme:

"Sing a song of sixpence,
A pocket full of rye;
Four-and-twenty blackbirds
Baked in a pie.
When the pie was opened,
The birds began to sing;
Wasn't that a dainty dish
To set before the King?"

TELL them you will open the pie after they have eaten. (The pie may be filled with favors for the guests.)

A Treasure Hunt Birthday Party

THE INVITATION

A SMALL ENVELOPE can be made into a Treasure Chest invitation.

CUT off the flap point, so it will look more like the edge of a chest cover, and cut the side folds.

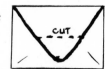

DRAW and paint a brass lock in the middle of the flap edge.

DRAW and color brown leather straps on each side—back and front—and make carrying handles on each end of the chest.

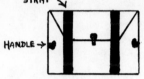

PRINT your invitation on the inside of the flap and envelope.

THE HUNT

EACH GUEST is given a list of clues to at least six places where directions are hidden. The last place will hold the treasure (or prize). Everyone must start at the same time.

DECORATIONS

THE TABLE DECORATION for a Treasure Hunt Party might be a "Money Tree."

USE a bare branch. Stand the bottom end in a box

(through a hole in the top). Cover the box with imitation paper money.

FASTEN candy coins to the branches with sticky tape or nylon thread.

Unusual Parties to Give

AN UP-SIDE-DOWN PARTY

THE INVITATIONS should be written up-side-down, and the guests might be asked to dress in the same mixed up style.

COME TO AN
UP-SIDE-DOWN
PARTY
AT
MARY BROWN'S
SATURDAY MAY 8th
AT
4 o'clock
DRESS UP-SIDE-DOWN

THE GAMES can be played up-side-down: A Potato Race may be arranged so the potatoes are not carried to a pail at the end of the row; instead, the player can be on his hands and knees rolling each potato to a given point, by pushing it with his nose. An Apple Eating contest would be amusing. Have each player seated on the floor and ask him to eat an apple without touching it with his hands.

SERVE REFRESHMENTS with all the plates up-side-down.

A Back-Side-To Party

THE INVITATION can be written backward, so it has to be held in front of a mirror to be read. Also ask the guests to come dressed backward.

THE GAMES can be played backward: with the players walking backward as they run a potato or peanut race; play musical chairs walking backward; play writing games and have the players write backward, or write from right to left.

THE REFRESHMENTS might be served backward too, with the ice cream coming first and the sandwiches last.

Novel Costume Parties

"COME AS YOU ARE": This unexpected invitation can bring some very amusing costumes.

A MAD HATTER PARTY: This calls for silly, amusing head-dresses or hats, and may bring guests wearing anything from a collection of kitchen gadgets to a duck blind.

A SPACE TRAVEL PARTY: Ask the guests to wear and bring what they think they should have if they were going to travel to outer space.

A SHIP WRECK PARTY: For this the guests dress as they might look had they been in a ship wreck.

Chapter 2

Summer Activities
Games to Play out of Doors
Hobbies and Things to Make

How to Play Scrub Baseball

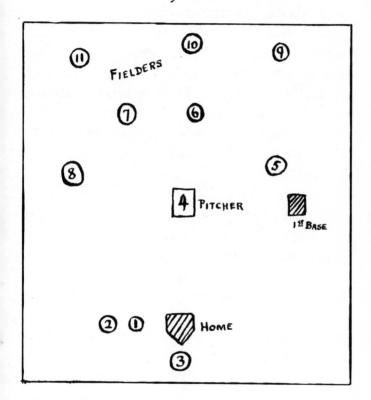

ABOVE is a diagram of the positions the players take in Scrub Baseball. The game needs only 6 players, but it is better to have 7, 8, or 9. As many as 11 can play.

THE DISTANCES between First Base, Home Plate, and the

Pitcher's Box vary according to the age, size, and speed of the players, as well as the weight of the ball. (Shorter distance for a soft ball.)

SCRUB 1 AND SCRUB 2 are at bat, and the object is to get a hit. They are temporary partners until one is put out. Scrub 3 is the Catcher. (The first batter after Scrub 2 is put out.) Scrub 4 is the Pitcher, Scrub 5 is on First Base, and the Fielders are placed according to the numbers: Second Base has Scrub 6, Shortshop Scrub 7, etc. Every player moves up to the next Scrub number when someone goes out of the Batter's Box. When either Scrub 1 or 2 is put out, he takes the field position that has the highest number.

THIS is the way the game goes: Scrub 1 and Scrub 2 are at bat. The object is to make a hit, run to First Base and if possible, run home. The player is out if a fly ball is caught, or if there is a grounder that is fielded to first base before the runner reaches it.

THERE is no scoring for the game. The fun is for everyone to try to get a turn at bat.

Counting Out
(Ways to choose the first player)

"BEE, bee, bumble bee, stung Aunt Betsy on the knee,

Stung her fat pig on the snout: 1—2—3—4, you are out."

"MY MOTHER won't let me play with you, so you are OUT!"

"RED, white, yellow, blue, all are out but Y-O-U."

"ONE, two, three, four, five, six, seven,
All good children go to Heaven.
One, two, three; out goes (he or she.)"

"AS I was walking down the street, I met a man with a keg of nails. How many nails were in the keg?" (The player pointed to gives a number, which is counted.)

How to Make a Bow and Arrow

MATERIALS: An old umbrella (one that will never be
used again)
Very strong string (nylon is best)
A small stick
A paring knife

THE UMBRELLA should be one that cannot be repaired, but it should have one unbroken rib that you can use.

TAKE out the rib and look at it carefully. You will find a small hole at each end.

TIE a strong string through each of these holes, making it tight so the rib will bend into a bow.

FOR AN ARROW, any small stick will do. Make a small slit in one end (with the paring knife), so it will slip over the string as you draw it back to shoot.

NOW before you try out this bow and arrow, go out of doors. Bows and arrows are not meant for indoor play. Also, watch where you shoot, for although the stick may not be pointed, it can hurt if it hits someone.

Racing Games

AN INDOOR OR OUTDOOR RACE: The players sit in a row, each one holding his left ankle with his right hand and his right ankle with his left hand. At a given signal the players move ahead to a given line, continuing to hold their ankles as they move.

A SACK RACE is fun. In this game each player runs or

hops along with both feet in a bag. Big burlap bags are best for this race, but heavy shopping bags will do. The race can also be played by tying each player's feet together with a wide strip of cloth, so he can take only short steps or will have to hop along.

LEAP FROG should have eight or ten players, the more players the better. The group forms two lines with each player squatting to make himself as small as he can. The last player in the line jumps over each of the squatting players in front of him and then he curls up at the head of the line. As soon as he reaches this position he shouts, "Go", and the player left at the end of the line gets up and jumps over the others the same way, finally squatting on the ground in front of the first player. The game continues this way until the first player is back at the end of the line in his original position. The line that finishes first is the winner.

Games to Play on the Holiday Picnic

RACES

THREE LEG RACE: The players race in pairs, with the right leg of one tied to the left leg of the other. (Be sure to use strips of cloth to tie the legs, because a rope will cut.)

WHEELBARROW RACE: The players race in pairs: One is the wheelbarrow and he has his hands on the ground, his feet out-stretched; the other is the driver of the wheelbarrow and he walks behind, holding the first player's legs. At a given signal they race across the field to a designated spot where they reverse positions—the wheelbarrow becomes the driver and the driver is the wheelbarrow. As soon as they have shifted positions, they race back to the starting point.

BACK TO BACK RACE: The players race in pairs. Each couple faces back to back and locks elbows. They race in one direction to a given line, and return to the start. On the return, they do not turn around but the player who has run backward races forward, and vice versa.

AN OBSTACLE RACE: As each participant must have the same obstacles on his race course, it may be necessary to run this in pairs. The obstacles used will depend on the location and things that are available or easy to move. Here are a few suggestions:

Something to crawl through—a large carton, a barrel, a hoop.

Jump over three or four boxes, logs, or stones.

Put on a silly costume—long skirt, large hat, sun glasses, mittens, etc. and put up an umbrella. Then the player might walk the length of a ladder, placed flat on the ground. Then remove the costume.

Set up a collapsed folding chair, sit in it, then fold
it up again.

Take off his shoes and socks, dip both feet in a pail
of water, wipe his feet on a towel, then put his
socks and shoes on again.

CONTESTS

JUMP THE DITCH: (This is a good game to play on a
beach picnic.) Lines are drawn about two feet apart, to
mark the ditch. The players line up and one by one jump
across the ditch. After each player has had a turn, the
ditch is made wider. The game continues this way and
when a player fails to jump across, he is out of the
contest.

The object is to see who can jump the widest ditch.

LEAF GATHERING: (This is a game for a picnic in the
woods.) See who can collect the largest variety of leaves
from the bushes and trees. He must have only one of
each species.

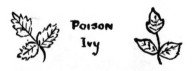

WARNING: Be sure every member of the party knows
poison ivy ("leaflet three, let it be"), so that is
avoided. Also, the leaves from wild flowers must

not be picked. It should be understood, during the leaf gathering, that each one must keep within sight or hearing distance of one another, or near "base operations."

STILL STICKS
(A quiet game to play on a holiday picnic)

GATHER 25 to 35 small sticks about 10″ long. They should be as straight and slender as possible, and stiff (not limp).

GRAB them as a handful and let them drop from the height of about two feet.

TAKE turns withdrawing one stick at a time. Each player may continue picking up the sticks until he makes a disturbing move and one in the pile stirs. He may use his hands, or one of the captured sticks, to flip off or lift another stick from the pile. As soon as he moves any of the adjacent sticks however, the next player takes his turn.

THE WINNER is the player that collects the most sticks.

A Summer Newspaper

IF you are staying in a summer resort, and no one else has started a local newspaper, you might write one. If possible, find someone to edit it with you, for it will require a lot of work and observation.

THE FIRST COPY should be especially good, so you will be able to get subscriptions after people read it. Don't try to make it too big, but have it a sheet of news that will be of interest to everyone, young and old. Keep a note book or pad of paper with you wherever you go, so you will be able to jot down news you find and items to report in your paper.

MATERIALS: A typewriter, paper, carbon, note pads, and plenty of pencils. A small note book—to keep track of your orders, and addresses of customers, as well as of your accounts, is essential.

SUGGESTED ITEMS FOR YOUR PAPER:
Title: "Summer Chatter"
Date: Month, day, year.
Your name and address: "Weekly news edited by ...."
Columns to include: "Whose News" — community or neighborhood news.
"What's Up"—coming events.
"Who Beat"—sports.
"Fish Story"—(check the catch)

"Junior Scoop"

"Arrivals and Departures"—
guests, comings and goings.

"Advertising"—Baby sitters, bait
for sale, rowing for flycasters,
etc.

Summer Activities

For the Whole Family

IN A small summer community it is fun to have various
family "get together" events. Here are a few suggestions:

Pet Show

Hobby Show

Evening community singing

Outdoor square dance

Amateur show for some worthy cause (Jimmy Fund,
etc.)

Field Day—with races, contests, and a baseball
game.

For Teen Agers

A SCAVENGER HUNT is always fun. The list of objects for
the hunt might differ according to the location, and the
age of the players. Before the players collect at a given

meeting place, make out as many lists of objects to find as will be needed. If it is a small group, the scavengers should go in pairs, but for a large gathering, have more in each group. Be sure to have a time limit when the scavengers must return with their collections.

Here are some suggested lists:

AT THE BEACH

    A square shaped stone
    A live crab (if possible)
    A star fish (if possible)
    A ship wreck object
    A perfectly round stone
    A lucky stone (with a ring around it)
    A green sea side flower
    A grotesque piece of driftwood
    A snail as small as a pea
    A picture of the sea
    A white egg-shaped stone
    Some part of a fish

IN THE COUNTRY

    A chicken feather
    A wish bone
    A piece of moss
    A mouse trap
    Hair from a horse's tail
    A vegetable resembling an animal
    A twig that looks like a fish
    6 varieties of leaves

A live fly
A small flag
A spoonful of sawdust
A year-old calendar

SUMMER TIME is a wonderful time to study the stars, especially if you are at the beach. Get a good book on astronomy at the library and take it on your vacation.

A Real Life Country Scene

WHEN you are vacationing in the country, it is fun to collect things to make a country scene.

YOU will need a shallow box or box top for your display. If you can find a small unframed mirror (pocket book size), this will be useful to represent water. Glue it to the inside of the box and plan your country scene around it.

COLLECT twigs, sticks, moss, pine needles, and tiny stones. If you know how to use a jack-knife, you might carve a duck, bird, or boat to add to your scene.

GLUE twigs together to make a log cabin; build a tiny stone wall; use pine twigs for trees; and add anything you can find in the woods that will make the scene look real.

Family Fun at the Sea Shore

BEACH scavenging is something the whole family can enjoy, especially if they make it a game. The best time to find treasures on the beach is after a storm. Take several days for the scavenging hunt, then when everyone is together, have the collections brought out to be displayed, admired, and laughed over. Here are suggestions for the things to collect on the beach:

The most grotesque.
The most beautiful.
The sweetest smelling.
The most valuable.
The most useful.
The most interesting.
The ugliest.
The oldest.

Decorating with Sea Shells

MATERIALS: Small sea shells
Snails
Dried star fish
Small dried crab
Sea urchins, etc.
Waterproof cement
A toothpick or small stick to apply the cement

The article you wish to decorate.

DECORATE any of the following articles with your seaside collections:

    A BASKET BAG, hand bag, or sewing basket.

    A HAT, either straw or cotton cloth.

    SHOES, straw or canvas.

    A FLAT BARETTE from the dime store.

    A PLAIN PLASTIC HEAD BAND—or a bicycle clip.

    EARRINGS, a plain clip or screw earring.

    TWIGS to make flowers for a table decoration.

    TOOTHPICKS for canapés. (Use the round picks.)

AFTER you have glued the shells, etc. to your article, paint the sea decoration with white shellac if you want it to shine and look more real—the way it shines when it is wet with sea water.

THE BAG and THE HAT can be decorated many ways. A piece of small colored net, a pearl glued to the open sea shell, or a piece of cork (use a cork stopple) cut and painted to represent a lobster buoy, all will help to make a conversation piece article.

Seaside Art Work

BUILD A PICTURE FROM A BEACH COLLECTION

MATERIALS: Heavy drawing paper, paste, blue water color paint and a brush or a blue crayon, and small things found on the beach: sand, sea weed, tiny rocks, shells, beach grass, wild beach flowers, and drift wood.

MAKE a picture with the above collection. First paint or crayon a sky. Next, cover the bottom of the paper with paste. Add sand to make a sandy beach. On this arrange your picture, placing the rocks, sea weed, and flowers where they will add to the scene. You will need more paste to hold them.

PAINT the water, waves, and a horizon line, before you paste on sand and the other articles, if you wish. There are many possibilities for making a sea side picture and it is fun to experiment.

CLAM SHELL PICTURES

Mount your favorite snap shot in a clam shell. Glue cot-

ton or a piece of felt to the inside of the shell first, to
make a flat backing for the picture.

A Rock Paper Weight or Door Stop

MATERIALS: a smooth white rock; plastic, oil, or enamel
paint, and a paint brush.

 PAINT a sea side scene on the rock. It will make an attractive paper weight or door stop.

Decorations for a Summer Dinner Party
(For a sea food dinner)

A FISH MOBILE might be made to suspend over the center
of the table. Make a lobster buoy from a round cereal

box. Cover it with red and white paper, and hang it over the table, from a light or the ceiling. Attach assorted lengths of fish line to the paper buoy, and at the end of each line, staple or paste a colorful paper fish.

CLAMSHELL PLACECARDS can be made by painting each guest's name on a shell. Use red enamel paint to match the lobster buoy.

CUCUMBER BOAT to hold olives or pickles: Cut a large cucumber lengthwise and scoop out the seeds, leaving a green shell. Make a mast and sail with a slender piece of carrot and a thin slice of bread cut into a triangle. Fasten these together with toothpicks.

Sandwich Markers for Your Summer Party

MATERIALS: Wooden ice cream spoons
Colored paint
A small paint brush
A small sharp knife
Sandpaper

CARVE each wooden handle into a point and sand it smooth.

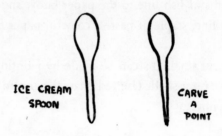

ICE CREAM
SPOON

CARVE
A
POINT

DECORATE the other end with a picture that will tell your guest what kind of sandwich you are serving. If you have a plate of sandwiches that can not be illustrated, print the name in fancy colored letters.

WHEN the sticks are finished, each one may be stuck into the top sandwich of a dish.

HERE are some illustrations:
  LOBSTER
  CRAB
  EGG
  HAM (a pig)
  FISH
  TOMATO
  CUCUMBER
  CHICKEN or TURKEY

THESE make a nice hostess gift.

Old Fashioned Pot Pourri

IN OLDEN DAYS on a table in most homes one would find a covered jar of a fragrant pot pourri. If the top of the jar is tight the aroma lasts for years.

MATERIALS needed to make two small jars of pot pourri:

> Four cups of dried rose petals
> One-half ounce allspice
> One-quarter ounce whole cloves
> One-half ounce stick cinnamon
> One-half ounce orris root
> Thin slivers of orange peel
> Four drops of oil of roses
> One-quarter cup brandy
> Salt

DRY the rose petals by spreading them out on a flat surface. Put the dried petals in a bowl, sprinkling them with salt as you add each layer. Do this as each batch of petals dries. Stir it up as you add a fresh lot. When you have enough dried petals, add the spices and let the mixture stand covered for a day or two. Then add the orris·root and fill the jars you want to use with the pot pourri, putting a little orange peel and brandy in each jar last.

SMALL glass candy jars with tight tops make attractive containers for the pot pourri. Tie a fancy ribbon around the neck of the jar.

A Jiffy-to-Make Kite

A HAND
DRILL

MATERIALS: Two yard sticks
A handdrill
A sheet of transparent plastic cloth (an
old plastic dress bag can be used)
A ball of twine
Some cellophane tape

DRILL a hole 9″ from the end of one yard stick, and drill another hole in the middle—18″ mark—of the other yard stick. Tie the two sticks together, crossed at these two holes. Have the tie string cross on the back and front as well as run through the holes, for the sticks must be fastened together securely.

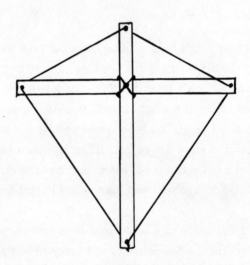

DRILL a hole ½″ from the ends of each stick. Then

thread a string through each hole, running it around the edge. (See illustration.)

COVER the kite skeleton with a sheet of the transparent plastic cloth. Lay the crossed sticks on the plastic and cut about 2″ from the string edge. Fold the plastic over the string and stick it down with tape. Be sure the plastic is stretched tight and smooth.

TIE a string across the cross strip, through the two end holes. Pull it tight and tie it to bow it, so the middle of the bow is about 7″.

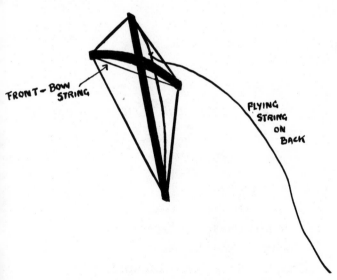

TIE a loose string to the top and bottom of the middle strip—through the two end holes, on the other side of the kite. Your kite flying string is tied to this, and it must be tied one-third of the way down from the top.

It is important to have the kite string attached at this exact point to balance it.

THE KITE STRING must be strong. Ask your dad if he has an old fish line you can use, for fish line is good and strong.

THIS KITE may be made of paper as well as plastic. If you have no cellophane tape, you can use glue, cement, or you can sew the covering on with nylon thread. If you use glue with plastic, be sure to test it on a sample piece of the plastic first, because some kinds of glue melt plastic.

Things to Take with You on Vacation

Your own list will vary according to the family interests.

FOR THE WHOLE FAMILY
> Two packs of playing cards
> Checkers, chess or cribbage set
> Games—"Scrabble," etc.
> Puzzles—jig-saw and cross-word
> Plenty of pencils and paper for playing games

FOR THE CHILDREN
> Cellophane tape

Glue, paste or cement
Scissors
Crayons or paints
Construction paper
Scratch paper
Story books

FOR THE BIRD WATCHER
Field glasses
A bird book

FOR THOSE WHO LIKE NATURE WALKS
A bird book
Book of sea shells
Book of wild flowers
Book of trees
A book about stars (astronomy)

FOR A HOUSEKEEPING COTTAGE VACATION
Take along some corn to pop. You do not need to have a corn popper. A covered frying pan can be used. If you have a rainy evening, this will help pass the time and entertain the children.

Chapter 3

Rainy and Stay-in-Bed Days

Things to Make
Games to Play Indoors

Some Things to Draw

MATERIALS: Drawing paper
A pencil or crayon

DRAW A CAT this way: First make a circle. On top make a half circle. Put on two ears. Add some whiskers. Then draw a tail.

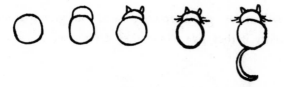

DRAW A SNOWMAN this way: First make a large circle. On top make a medium-sized circle. Put on a smaller circle. Add two arms. Make some eyes, a nose and a mouth. Give it a hat, and some round buttons.

More Things to Draw

A LIFE SIZE PICTURE is fun to draw.

MATERIALS: A very large sheet of wrapping paper and
            crayons

SPREAD the wrapping paper on the floor—not on a rug.
Then lie on your back on the paper. Keep your arms
away from your body and lie very still while someone
draws around you.

WHEN your outline has been drawn, color the picture
so it will look like you.

THIS will make a good present to send your grandparents,
especially if they live where they cannot see you often.

Life Pictures

MATERIALS: A very large sheet of cardboard
            A pencil
            Poster paints
            Sharp scissors

DRAW and then paint on the cardboard a picture of some
animal; person, or character you would like to be. Make

just a round circle for the head, hands and feet. When the picture is done, cut out these circles.

STAND behind the cardboard picture and put your head in the hole where the character's head should be. Put your hands through the holes where the hands should be, and let your toes show through the holes where the feet go.

A Sugar Lump House

MATERIALS: Lump (or cubed) sugar
Confectioners' sugar

Water
Small butter knife
Sheet of white construction paper
Vegetable coloring
A cookie sheet

MAKE a frosting paste of the powdered sugar and water, and use this to stick the cubes of sugar together.

DESIGN the four walls of the house, building them in four separate sections, flat on the cookie sheet. (This enables you to leave spaces for a door and windows.) Use only enough frosting paste to hold the cubes together. Make the walls four or five cubes high and five or seven cubes wide—depending on the number of windows you want.

WHEN the frosting paste has dried thoroughly, lift each section carefully and stand the four walls together, pasting them to form the house.

THE ROOF is made of construction paper. Cut it a little wider than the front of the house, and long enough to fold in the middle and rest on the front and back walls.

FILL in the opening at the two sides of the house—under the roof, with more lumps of sugar. Break the lumps to fit, and use frosting paste to hold them.

THE CHIMNEY may be made of two sugar cubes (or a lump broken in half) pasted to the roof.

Recipes for the Home Craftsman

HOME MADE PASTE: Make a thick paste of flour and water. Add enough boiling water to make it creamy and then stir in a few drops of oil of wintergreen. This will help to keep it from growing sour.

> PASTE STICKS: A wooden ice-cream spoon makes a good paste stick.

HOME MADE MODELLING CLAY: Mix together 4 tablespoons of cornstarch, 8 tablespoons of salt and 8 tablespoons of boiling water. Mix them in order and stir until the dough forms a ball. Knead with your fingers for a few minutes. If it is crumbly, add more water. If it is too sticky, put in more starch. If you want to color the clay, add the coloring with the water. (Use vegetable coloring.)

> ANOTHER modelling wax can be made by mixing soap powder with enough water to make it the consistency of clay.

FINGER PAINT: Add ½ cup soap flakes to 1 pint of hot creamy boiled laundry starch. Mix thoroughly. Put a little in each cup of a muffin pan and add vegetable coloring. (The recipe for boiled starch is on the package of powdered laundry starch.)

PAPIER-MACHE: (Used to model dolls and animals.) Cut newspaper into pieces small enough to roll into balls. Put these in a kettle of boiling water and cook for about 10 minutes. Pour off the water and add 8 tablespoons of laundry starch and the white of 2 eggs for each quart of paper. Work this mixture with your hands and mold into the desired shape.

Bed Tray Occupations

TRY writing a letter with the paper in front of a mirror. Do not look directly at the paper but view it only through the mirror.

WRITE your name backward so you can read it facing your mirror.

TAKE a piece of string ten inches long and see how many

pictures you can make with it by just placing it in different positions on a sheet of paper.

PAPER CLIPS can be used to make designs and pictures. They also are fun to link together to make bracelets and chains.

SCRAP BAG PICTURES: Small pieces of colored cloth and scraps of yarn can be cut up to make designs and flowers. Paste these on paper so you can save the picture.

An Indoor Bow and Arrow

MATERIALS: A pencil

A large elastic
A small piece of cardboard

THIS bow and arrow is perfectly safe to use indoors.

CUT the cardboard in the shape of an arrow, but do not make it less then an inch in width. Notch one end of it and cut the other end into a point.

NOW to shoot the arrow, wind the elastic around a pencil twice, hook the arrow through the loop of the second wind of elastic—with the notched end of the arrow pulling the elastic.

PULL back the arrow, stretching the elastic, then let it go.

A Spool Pistol

MATERIALS: A large spool
Two elastic bands (one should be strong and thick)

A thin stick—that will slip through the hole in the spool

CUT the thick elastic band and fasten the two ends to the sides of the spool—by winding another elastic around it.

TO SHOOT the pistol, put the small stick through the hole in the spool and pull it out with the elastic behind it—stretching the elastic as much as you can.

LET the stick go and it will shoot out of the spool like a pistol shot.

THIS is a good gun to use in shooting toy soldiers.

A Hand Puppet

MATERIALS: A colored handerchief
Two black ball-shaped buttons (shoe buttons)
A white button
A red button

DOUBLE up your fist and put the two black buttons in the crack between the little finger and the ring finger—one on each side of the knuckle. In the crack between the next two fingers put the white button—just under the knuckle. In the last crack put the red button—for the mouth.

NOW that you have made the face, drape a hankie (or scarf) over the fist. Tie it like a kerchief.

IF you would like some nice red cheeks, paint them with lipstick.

Make a Stencil

DRAW the picture you want to stencil on heavy construction paper. Make it something that has a clear outline—such as a leaf, an animal, a tree, or a flower.

PUSH the point of your scissors through the center of the picture and from this hole start to cut out the drawing. Be careful to cut only just inside the outline, not beyond the edge of the picture.

WHEN you have finished cutting out the picture you will have a frame left. This is your stencil.

TO USE IT place the frame on a clean sheet of paper and color inside the stencil.

IF you want to copy a picture to use for your stencil, cover it with a sheet of paper that is firm but thin enough to see through and draw the outline of the object. Place the tracing, drawing side down, on a sheet of construction paper and trace the lines of the drawing. This will give you a copy to cut for a stencil.

A Circus Mobile

MATERIALS: Construction or drawing paper
A ball of string
Crayons
Scissors
A pencil
A pin
Paste

CUT a large half-circle from the construction paper, then

spread paste halfway down the straight edge, and roll
the circle so the other half of that edge rests under the
paste. (See illustration.) This is the circus tent.

PASTE

DRAW and color circus animals, a clown, a tightrope
walker, or a circus lady.

CUT OUT the figures and color the backs the same as the
fronts.

PRICK a hole in the top of each circus figure and thread
a string through the hole. Tie a knot in one end of the
string and thread the other end through a pricked hole
on the edge of the circus tent. Make a knot in that
end too.

TIE all the circus figures to the edge of the tent the same

way, then thread a string through the top of the tent—
tying a knot in the end on the inside of the tent.

THUMBTACK the string that comes from the top of the
tent to the top of the door frame.

Animals Made from Envelopes

MATERIALS: Strong envelopes all sizes—the large 11″
by 4¾″ are best—a pencil, and scissors.

IF the envelopes have been through the mail be sure they
are still firm and not torn.

COLLECT pictures of animals to use for models.

USING the bottom edge of the envelope for the animal's
back, draw a side view of it on the front of the envelope.
See illustration.

CUT out the head, rear end, and feet of the animal, but
do not cut where the top of the head and the tail touch
the folded edge.

  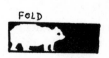 

SPREAD the legs of the animal and he will stand up.

IF you want colored animals, crayon or paint them before you cut them out.

A 3-D Picture

3-D means "3 dimension." That is, not flat, but a picture in which all the figures stand out and look lifelike.

MATERIALS: A large piece of white paper, (drawing, shelf, or wrapping paper)
Colored tissue or crepe paper
Colored construction paper
Paste
Scissors

TO MAKE a 3-D picture, cut out figures (flowers, trees, houses and grass), and paste each one to the big sheet of paper. BUT do not paste these cut out pieces *flat*. Only part of each piece is pasted.

FOR GRASS use a long narrow strip of green crepe paper and paste it in waves across the bottom of the picture. (See illustration.)

FLOWERS should be pasted in the center of the back—leaving the petals loose so they will fold out.

UILDINGS will stand out if they are cut with side flaps
at can be folded under and pasted to the picture.

EOPLE added to the picture may be pasted so the arms,
ead, and legs are free. Or a small tab of paper—folded
n half—can be pasted with one end fastened to the back
f the figure and the other to the picture.

A Paper Clown

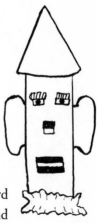

IATERIALS: Toilet paper roll
White drawing paper
Colored crepe paper or tissue paper
Crayons
Scissors
Paste

VRAP a piece of drawing paper around the cardboard
oll and mark where to cut it so it will fit the roll and

overlap a little at the back. (Overlap enough to paste—
but do not paste yet.)

A FACE for the clown should be made in the middle of
the paper you have just fitted to the roll. This face is cut
so the eyelashes will fold forward, the nose turn up, and
the lips fold over. When these have been cut, color the
lips red and make a red spot on each cheek. Fringe the
eyelashes by cutting several slits in them after they have
been colored.

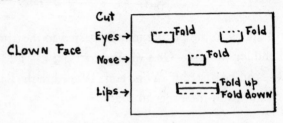

paste the face-piece to the paper roll and color eyes inside the two eye openings.

CUT a strip of colored tissue paper and, after you have
put paste around the bottom edge of the clown head,
ruffle it as you paste it around the neck of the clown, to
make a collar.

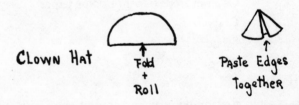

MAKE a clown hat from a rolled up half circle of paper

nd if you like, add ears to the head, cutting them with
flap at the back so they can be pasted to the clown's
:ad.

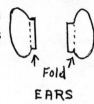

A Motor for Your Boat

:Y this with your small bath tub boat that has no motor.

\STEN a piece of camphor to the back of the boat. Be
ıre to fasten it low enough to touch the water and use
rong water-proof glue to fasten the camphor.

IE GLUE should be thoroughly dry before the boat is
ıt in the water.

ND THEN watch it go!

A Yarn Bracelet

ATERIALS: Colored yarn
White cotton thread

Needle
Scissors

CUT eighteen strands of the yarn eighteen inches long

TIE these pieces together two inches from one end—by
wrapping a short strip of yarn around the pieces twice
and tying it tight. Leave the ends two inches long to
match the ends of the other pieces.

DIVIDE the eighteen strands of yarn into three part
(three groups of six pieces) and braid them. The easiest
way to do this is to pin the top end to something—the
arm of a stuffed chair or couch. Braid to within two
inches of the end, then wrap a piece of yarn around the
threads and tie it as you did at the other end.

MAKE a doll at each end: First make a head, by tying
yarn around the pieces ½ inch below the tie at the end
of the braid, leaving ends the length of the others.

FOR ARMS separate three strands each side, below the
head, and braid them. Tie a piece of yarn to hold the
braid together at the wrist of the doll.

NEXT tie yarn around the remaining ends—at the doll'
waist. This will make a girl doll.

AT THE OTHER END of the braid, work the same way, but
divide the threads in half below the doll's waist and tie

them together to make two feet. This will make a boy doll.

MAKE the dolls' faces by sewing eyes, nose and mouth with white cotton thread.

THIS fancy band can be tied around the wrist for a bracelet. If you would like to wear it around your neck, cut the eighteen strands of thread longer (about thirty inches in all.)

A Doll's Scarf

MATERIALS: Ribbon 1″ wide and as long as you want the scarf (this will depend on the size of the doll)
Yarn to match the ribbon
A small crochet hook
Needle
Thread
Scissors

TURN UP each end of the ribbon about ¼ inch, then turn the ends over again the same distance, so the ragged edges do not show.

BASTE this folded edge down enough to hold it in place.

(To baste, have a knot in the end of the thread, and take stitches that can be pulled out later.)

 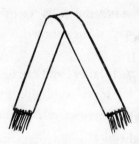

TO MAKE a fringe on the ends of the scarf, cut several strips of yearn two inches long. Then using the crochet hook, and working on the right side of the scarf, pierce through the ribbon just above the folded edge and hook a strip of yarn (folded in the middle.) Bring the hooked yarn through the ribbon just far enough so that the two ends on the other side can slip through the loop. Make a fringe this way across each end of the scarf.

THE BASTING should be pulled out after the fringe is made.

A Doll's Bedspread

MATERIALS: Sheeting (unbleached if possible)
Yarn or heavy embroidery silk
An embroidery needle

Crayons
Scissors
Heavy paper

CUT the sheeting the size you want your doll's spread.
If it is wrinkled, be sure to press it before you take the
next step.

DECORATE THE SPREAD: Lay the cloth flat on a table or
the floor—not on a rug—and using colored crayons,
draw a picture or design in the middle and at each corner
of the material. In order to repeat the same design, it is
best to cut a pattern from heavy paper, then color inside
the cut out design. (Fold the paper twice, like a hankie,
and cut a quarter of the pattern. When you open the
paper, it will have a stencil for you to use.)

AFTER you have finished coloring the design on your
bedspread, press the material again, ironing over the
crayoned design.

TO FINISH THE EDGE: Use yarn or heavy embroidery silk
and a big needle. Make a knot in the end of your thread,
then overcast all the way around the cloth.

HOW TO OVERCAST: Put the threaded needle through the
cloth close to the edge on the wrong side, bringing it out
on the right side. Then put the needle through the cloth
again on the wrong side—this time about a half inch
from where it went in before. Make these stitches all

around the edge of the spread. If you will remember to always put the needle into the cloth on the wrong side and pull it out on the right, and keep the stitches the same distance apart and close to the edge, it will make a very pretty finish on the edge of the spread.

TO FASTEN the end of each thread, run the needle under the last two or three stitches on the wrong side, then cut off the thread. Begin a new length of thread by having a knot in the end and by putting the needle through the cloth where you would have taken the next stitch.

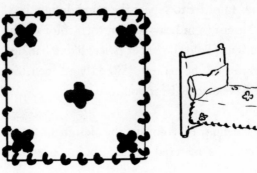

Fun with Camphor

MATERIALS: Three or four flat cakes of camphor
             Glue or cement
             Paper
             Crayons
             Scissors

A shallow dish of water

DRAW, color, and cut out small objects. Glue each one to the top of a camphor cake, then float the cake in a dish of water and watch it move.

MAKE a stand for each object so it can be pasted upright on the camphor cake. (Use a small strip of paper and paste it to the back of the object—leaving it long enough to fold over at the bottom—so it can be pasted to the cake of camphor.)

TRY it with the following objects:
Children dancing
Children skating
Sailboats
Flags
Circus animals
Autos

A Loom for Weaving

MATERIALS: An old picture frame—or narrow strips of wood to make your own frame. (Nail four strips of wood together, being sure to have the top and bottom strips the same length, and the two side strips the same length. (See illustration.)

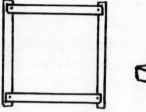 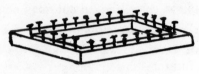

NOW using inch-long nails, fasten a row of nails into the top and bottom edges of the frame, pounding them into the wood only deep enough to make them stay firm. Have the nails an equal distance apart (about ¼ inch.) Next put nails into the side edges of the frame in the same way.

Hand Woven Articles

(The loom just described is used for this weaving.)

TO WIND THE LOOM: Use heavy knitting or crocheting yarn. Tie the end of the ball of yarn to the first nail on the bottom edge of the frame. Then going back and forth from top to bottom, wind the yarn around the nails on the two opposite edges. Keep the lines of yarn straight and tight. When the last nail is reached, tie the thread to it and cut off the yarn.

TO WEAVE: Cut a piece of yarn about a yard long. Tie one end to the top nail on the left side of the frame and thread the other end through a tape needle (or a big needle with a blunt end.) Now run the needle first over and then under the up and down threads, pulling the yarn across the frame. Next wind the yarn over the top nail on the rightside and weave the yarn back over the threads—this time going under where the last weave went over. Weave back and forth from side to side, at the end of each row going around a nail, until the bottom nail on each side has been wound. If a new thread has to be added, attach it on a side, at a nail.

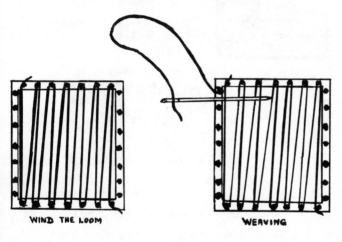

WIND THE LOOM   WEAVING

FINISH the end by tying the thread to the loop around the next nail. Then untie the knot you made at the beginning and tie that end to the loop around the nail next to it.

TO TAKE the woven mat from the frame, slip the loops off the nails, one at a time, being careful not to stretch the weaving out of shape.

THINGS TO MAKE ON THIS LOOM

Doll or baby blankets, a scarf, or tablemats, can all be made from the woven pieces made on this loom.

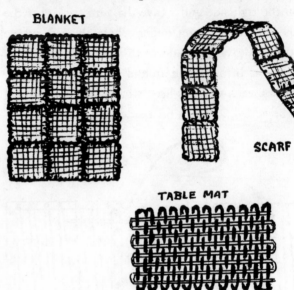

BLANKET

SCARF

TABLE MAT

THE BLANKET AND SCARF are both made by sewing the woven pieces together with yarn of the same color, using a blunt needle. Join the pieces by sewing through the side loops. First fasten the end of your yarn by tying it to the first loop, then weave back and forth through the loops on the sides of the pieces. Begin with the top side loop and work down to the bottom, tying the yarn from your needle to the last loop.

THE TABLE MATS should be woven with cotton yarn or cord.

A Bead Doll Book Mark

MATERIALS: Colored beads (three large, two medium
     sized white ones, and twenty-eight small)
     Heavy embroidery cotton
     A needle
     Scissors

CUT four lengths of the embroidery cotton, each one
fourteen inches long.

HOLDING the four threads together evenly, tie one knot
2½ inches from each end, another knot in the middle of
the group of threads, and then another halfway between
the center and each end knot.

TO MAKE THE GIRL DOLL: Sew the four threads on one
end through one of the white, medium sized beads. Make
a knot to hold the bead. Then divide the threads, sewing
one on each side through four small beads (for arms).
Tie a knot in each end to hold the beads.

NEXT sew the two middle threads through the two large
beads (to make a body), and make a knot in *each* thread
to hold the beads. Now sew each thread separately
through three small beads (to make feet). Tie a knot
in each end to hold the beads.

TO MAKE THE BOY DOLL: Sew the threads on the other
end through beads, using the same order except for the

body and legs. One bead makes the boy's body and five beads should be used for each leg.

IF an end of thread is left at any of the arms or legs, cut it off after you are sure the knot is secure.

FACES can be made on each doll by using a toothpick and painting eyes, nose, and a mouth with nail polish.

Small Fringed Napkins

MATERIALS: ¼ yard linen 36″ wide
Thread to match
Needle
Textile paint
Scissors

CUT the linen into four nine-inch squares. Cut on a thread so all the sides are perfectly even.

STITCH ½ inch from the edge all the way around each square. Be careful to stitch straight lines even with the threads.

RAVEL the loose threads outside the stitching around each napkin edge.

PAINT a design in one corner of each napkin. The best way to do this is to sketch your design first, then trace the sketch lightly over carbon paper so it will be printed faintly on the napkin. Apply the textile paint either with a small brush or straight from the tube if it comes in a tube with a ball point.

PLAN your design so all four napkins make a complete set. For Christmas make a tree, wreath, bell, Santa, or candy cane; summer napkins might have a boat, crab, star fish, or lobster; and for spring napkins use flower designs.

Make Your Own Earrings

VERY unusual earrings can be made from antique, fancy buttons found in Grandmother's button box. Plain, clip, or screw type earrings can be bought for a small sum, and with water-proof cement, all sorts of ornaments can be added to make the earrings. Here are a few suggestions:

Old buttons
Sea shells
Beads
Pine cones
Felt cut-outs
Tiny china figures

Pine Cones

Buttons

Applique

TO MAKE the following appliqués, one cuts figures from one piece of material and uses them to decorate another material. There are different ways to fasten the pieces to be appliquéd:

WITH LEATHER, FELT AND FUR, use fabric cement—being sure it is a make that will not stain the material. Work on a clean flat surface covered with white paper as you cement the figure to the fabric. After the cement has dried, the figure should be fastened more securely by overcasting the raw edges and sewing through both materials.

WHEN CLOTH figures are appliquéed, the raw edges

should be turned under and basted down, then sewed to the material.

THINGS TO APPLIQUE

A FELT SKIRT is fun to appliqué. Use figures cut from contrasting colored felt. A child's felt skirt with a colored alphabet or animals appliquéed on it will delight any little girl. An adult skirt might be decorated with flowers, a design or figures to represent her hobby.

A FELT APRON of Christmas red might be appliquéed for the holiday. Sew on a green felt tree and wreaths, silver bells, tiny gold stars, an angel, a snowman, and a candy cane.

CURTAINS AND A BEDSPREAD for a child's room are fun to appliqué. Use unbleached sheeting that has been washed and thoroughly shrunk. Sew on nursery rhyme figures or animals cut from colored cloth. See illustration of figures for these.

Stamp a Design

MATERIALS: Thick poster paint
Small objects to use as stamps
A muffin tin or several small saucers
Sheets of newspaper
The paper to be decorated

COLLECT the objects you will use for stamps. You will find them right in our own house. Here are a few:

    an empty spool
    a thimble

  a bottle cork
  a button
  a bottle cap
  a large screw
  a pencil

POUR a little poster paint into each cup of the muffin tin. Spread your paper to be decorated on several sheets of newspaper. Dip the top of the object you are using for a stamp in one of the colors of paint and then press it on the paper.

USE the different shapes and colors to make up your design.

To Amuse the Stay-in-Bed

ALL YOU NEED to do these puzzles and games is a pencil and paper.

HOW MANY WORDS can you make from the letters in each of the following words?

DICTIONARY

ALPHABET
IMAGINARY
PERSONALITY

HOW MANY WORDS can you name that have more than one meaning? Example: do—due—dew.

HOW MANY WORDS can you name that make a word if spelt backward? Example: trap—part.

HOW MANY ANIMALS can you name that begin with the letter "C?"

HOW MANY THINGS TO EAT can you name that begin with the letter "B?"

HOW MANY ARTICLES OF CLOTHING can you name that begin with the letter "S?"

More Games for the Stay-in-Bed

HOW FAR CAN YOU GO in the alphabet naming articles of clothing that begin with each letter? Start with A and use the letters in order.

LIST everything in the room beginning with the letter B.

HOW MANY BOY'S NAMES can you list beginning with the letter C?

HOW MANY GIRLS' NAMES can you list beginning with the letter D?

GO THROUGH THE ALPHABET and see if you can make a sentence with the same letter beginning each word. For example, using the letter B: "Busy Betsy Buzzed Briskly By Barbara's Bus."

WRITE the numbers 1   2   3 on a large sheet of paper, making each one a good size. Now see what three pictures you can draw using the line of the number in each picture. See illustration.

Thinking of a Number
(A game for two people to play)

MATERIALS: Pencils and a paper chart for each player.

THE CHART should be marked with lines to divide it into ten columns. The heading of each column has a number and they should read from 1 to 10.

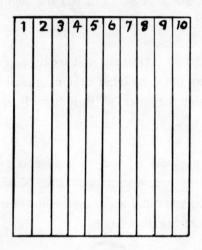

CHOOSE which one is to be the first player—toss a penny, or count out.

THE FIRST PLAYER puts his pencil on one of the numbers on his chart (without letting the other player see.)

"THINKING OF A NUMBER" is what he says.

THE SECOND PLAYER guesses a number. If he does not guess the right one, the first player can write on his chart the number he named—putting it in the column headed by that number. The second player keeps on guessing until he names the right number, and each time the first player writes down the wrong guesses. But if the number is guessed correctly, the other player can write it down *on his* chart and it will be *his* turn to think of a number. He does not have a turn until he guesses correctly, but the first player cannot change the number he started with. The game continues until one of the players has filled all ten columns. (Each column must have at least five numbers.)

Hickory Dickory Dock Game
(For two players)

MATERIALS: Paper and pencils.

DRAW a clock face on each player's paper. The face should be at least three inches wide.

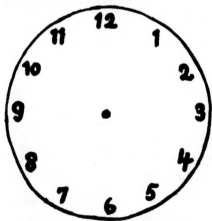

THE FIRST PLAYER closes his eyes (no peeking), and circles his pencil over the face of the clock—not marking on it. While he does this, he says:

> "Hickory dickory dock,
>> The mouse ran up the clock.
>> The clock struck ...."

AFTER the word "struck" he drops his pencil-point to the clock, opens his eyes and looks to see what number is nearest the place his pencil touches. That number is marked out.

NOW the second player does the same with his clock face and each player takes turns marking out numbers. If the pencil marks numbers that have been used, no score is made.

THE OBJECT of the game is to see which clock has all the numbers marked first.

A Dart Game

MATERIALS: A large piece of cloth (an old sheet)
                 Crayons
                 Several cork stoppers
                 Some straight pins

A TARGET should be drawn and colored on the piece of cloth. Make it any size you like. There should be a star in the center, and around that several circles. Use a bright red crayon to draw the target and make the star any color you want.

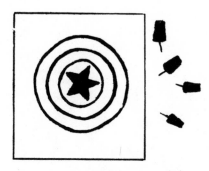

THE DARTS are made from cork stoppers. Push a straight pin—head first—into the larger end of the cork. Leave the point sticking out.

WHEN you throw the darts at the cloth target, the pin will stick to the spot it hits. Pin your target to a pillow and stand the pillow on the floor, against a couch or stuffed chair. Drape the rest of the sheet over the furniture behind it. (This will be protection in case some of the darts go astray.)

THROW the darts as you sit on the floor opposite the target. Throw a few to test the distance you should be from the target.

Chapter 4

Holiday Greeting Cards

Spray and Spatter Painting Greeting Cards

MATERIALS: White or colored construction paper
Gold, white, or colored poster paint
Scissors
A small water color paint brush
If you are spraying your card, you will need a bottle with a spray attachment. For spattering a card, use an old sieve and a water color paint brush. (The paint is spattered through the sieve with the paint brush.)

CUT the figure you want to use from heavy paper. Use either the cut out figure, or the paper from which the figure was cut, for your pattern.

YOUR CARD should be cut from construction paper. If you make a white card, you can use any color paint for the spray. On a colored card, spatter white or gold paint.

SPRAY or spatter paint around or inside the paper pattern, as it rests on your card. Remove the pattern and you will find an outline of it.

PRINT your message on or beside the figure.

HERE are suggestions of patterns to use on a spattered or sprayed greeting card:

> For someone taking a trip: boat, plane, suitcase
> For parents of a new baby: cradle, carriage, a stork carrying a baby
> Anniversary: bell, two rings, the date of the marriage
> Birthday: cake with candles
> Christmas: tree, Santa with pack, bells, wreath
> Easter: a cross, stained glass church window
> Someone with a new house: moving van, house
> Valentine's day: a heart with an arrow through it

A Cut Out Greeting Card

CUT OUT parts of your illustrated greeting card, and glue colored tissue paper behind the cut out. If you do not want it to show on the back side, cut two pieces exactly alike, and glue the tissue paper between them. Try it with these cards:

A Church Window for Easter

CUT THE window into sections (like a stained glass window), and use a different color tissue paper in each section. Or, brush tissue paper with assorted colors of paint. This will make it look like stained glass.

EASTER GREETINGS

An Easter Cross

CUT out the cross and use gold or yellow paper.

A House

MAKE it a night scene. Cut out the windows, and use yellow paper to make it look as if the lights were on in the house.

A Christmas Tree

USE colored paper for the lights and ornaments.

Family Picture Greeting Cards

MATERIALS: A snapshot of each member of the family
               Construction paper
               Watercolor paints
               Scissors
               Paste

CUT the card from white construction paper, making it single or double, depending on the length of the message you plan to send.

FROM green paper cut a Christmas tree. Make it large enough to cover most of the front of the card. (The size will depend on the number of pictures you use.)

CUT OUT a picture of each member of the family, outlining the head, or circling around it.

DRAW a star pattern large enough to hold the picture, and cut a star to go with each of the family pictures. These stars may be made from gold, yellow, or white paper. (If you use white paper, paint it yellow or gold.)

PASTE a head snapshot in the center of each star, and then paste the star to the tree.

PRINT a greeting on the card, and print the name of each person under the star holding his picture.

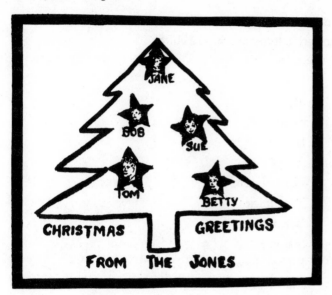

ANOTHER FAMILY CARD might be made by drawing a picture of your house, and having the cutout snapshot of each person at a window.

An Illustrated Letter
(A greeting for a child)

CHILDREN are always delighted with an illustrated letter. If you cannot draw the illustrations yourself, cut them from magazines, or use real articles. Write a poem to go with the objects, or make up a story about them. Here

are a few suggestions of things that might be fastened
to such a letter to amuse a child:

- Penny
- Life-saver
- Elastic
- Paper clip
- Balloon
- Safety pin
- Piece of gum
- Toothpick
- Button
- Stamp
- Ribbon bow
- Candy pill
- Paper doll
- Band aid
- Small flag
- Colored pipe cleaner

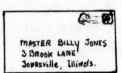

Greeting Cards Made with Real Objects

SOME of the most attractive greeting cards are designed
to use real objects. Here are a few ideas to work on:

A SPRIG OF HOLLY, tied to a card, makes a pretty Christmas greeting.

A COIN, glued to a card, with an appropriate rhyme, is something amusing.

"Here's a penny for your thoughts.
Why don't you write?"

A STICK OF GUM, attached to a card, will please a child.

A REAL FEATHER might be used on a picture of an Easter bonnet.

A BOOK MARK, made of felt or ribbon, could be used on a "get well quick" card.

BABY BOOTIES made from felt or yarn (doll size), tied together on a card, make an attractive greeting for a new mother.

Birthday Cards

IF you are making a birthday card, you might illustrate
it with the flower of that month. Here are the flowers
for each month:

> January—carnation or snowdrop
> February—violet
> March—daffodil or jonquil
> April—daisy or sweet pea
> May—lily of the valley
> June—rose or honeysuckle
> July—larkspur
> August—poppy or gladioli
> September—aster
> October—calendula or cosmos
> November—chrysanthemum
> December—holly or narcissus

Folded Tree Greeting Card

MATERIALS: Heavy white construction paper
            Green gift-wrap paper
            Green ink (or water color paint)
            Silver or gold glitter
            Glue

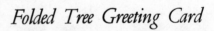

CUT a triangular pattern 5 inches tall and with a 4½
inch base.

PLACE this pattern in the middle of the white paper and draw around it. Place the same pattern beside the drawing, with the points together and one 5 inch side even with the 5 inch side of the drawing. Draw around the pattern. Now place the pattern on the opposite side of the first triangle, with the points together and a 5 inch side even with the other and draw around the pattern.

CUT OUT this three triangle drawing.

CUT a triangle from the green paper the same size as the pattern.

FOLD the three triangles along the 5 inch inside lines so the triangles are on top of one another.

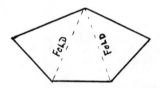

GLUE the green triangle to the front of the folded card and decorate it with glitter by dropping spots of glue on the green and scattering glitter over them.

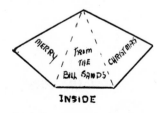

OUTSIDE   **INSIDE**

WITH green ink write your greeting and name on the inside of the card.

Days to Send Greeting Cards

New Years' Day—January 1st
Valentine's Day—February 14th
St. Patrick's Day—March 17th
April Fool's Day—April 1st
Easter—differs each year
Mother's Day—first Sunday in May
Graduation Day
Father's Day—usually the 3rd Sunday in June
Halloween—October 31st
Thanksgiving—usually the last Thursday in November
Christmas—December 25th
Birthdays
Anniversaries
Congratulations—for a new baby, etc.
To a sick friend
Someone taking a trip
Friends in a new home

Wedding Anniversary Cards

IF you know what year the couple are celebrating, it is

nice to use that when you are illustrating an anniversary
card. Here is a list of wedding anniversaries:

First—Paper and Plastic

Second—Cotton

Third—Leather

Fourth—Books, Silk, Fruit

Fifth—Wood

Sixth—Iron

Seventh—Copper, Wool, Brass

Eighth—Bronze, Electric

Ninth—Pottery

Tenth—Tin, Aluminum

Eleventh—Steel

Twelfth—Silk, Linen

Thirteenth—Lace

Fourteenth—Ivory

Fifteenth—Crystal

Twentieth—China

Twenty-fifth—Silver

Thirtieth—Pearl

Thirty-fifth—Coral, Jade

Fortieth—Ruby

Forty-fifth—Sapphire

Fiftieth—Gold

Fifty-fifth—Emerald

Sixtieth—Diamond

Chapter 5

Family Games
Car Games
Party Games
Games to Play Alone

Drawing Lots

WITH DICE—Each player has a turn tossing the dice. The winner tosses the highest number.

WITH CARDS—Each player draws one card from a pack. The winner draws the highest card.

WITH A PENNY—(This can be used with two players only.) One player tosses the penny and, while it is in the air, the other player names either, "Heads" or "Tails." If the penny lands with what he has called on the top side, he wins.

WITH A STICK—Each player throws a stick and the one who throws the farthest is the winner.

SCRUB ONE—When a game is to be played, the first to say, "Scrub one" is the winner. (In baseball he is the first man at the bat.)

WITH STRAWS—Break a straw or stick into the same number of pieces as there are players. Make each piece a different length. One person offers them for choice to the others. They should be grouped together and held in one hand, placed so they appear to be all the same length.

Then each player selects a straw and the winner is declared to be the one with the shortest (or longest). This could even be the player who held the straws.

Forfeits
(An indoor or outdoor game)

FORFEITS can be played with any number of people. Each player puts some article of his (or hers) in a collection pile: a ring, pin, tie, shoe, watch, sweater, etc.

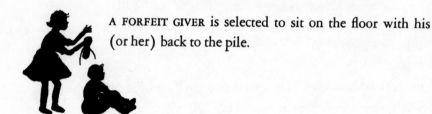

A FORFEIT GIVER is selected to sit on the floor with his (or her) back to the pile.

ANOTHER PLAYER is chosen to distribute the articles. This person selects an article from the pile and holds it over the Forfeit Giver's head (so the latter can not see it) while these lines are repeated:

"Heavy, heavy, hangs over your head.

What shall the owner do to redeem it?"

THE FORFEIT GIVER decides what shall be done and the owner of the article must carry out the order. None of the forfeits are performed until all the articles have been redeemed. The Forfeit Giver will be deciding his own forfeit without knowing it.

HERE ARE SOME GOOD FORFEITS:
    Stand on one foot while you count to fifty.
    Kiss the bottom of each foot.
    Roll a bottle across the room with your nose.
    Say the alphabet backward.
    Sing a song, or say a poem.

Family Games

FLIP THE CARDS—Place a pan or bowl in the center of the room and let each person try to flip a dozen playing cards into it as he stands four feet away.

BOUNCE—Try to bounce a ball into a pail or basket. The player must stand ten to twelve feet from the basket and bounce the ball on the floor once before it jumps into the basket.

RING TOSS—Cut out the centers of six or eight paper plates and use the rims as rings to toss over the top of a tall bottle.

PANTOMINES—In the evening it is fun for the family to play the game of telling what each one has done during the day, without speaking, but using pantomine: Mother gestures to show what she did during the day, or little sister uses movements to describe her activities. The rest of the family tries to guess what is being described by the gestures.

TELL A STORY—One person starts the story, but when he says "and" the next one goes on with it. Each person adds to it as his turn to start follows an "and." This can continue around the group as many times as the interest holds.

How to Play "Yap"
(A dice game for two or more players)

MATERIALS: Five dice and a dice cup, paper and pencils for each player.

EACH player has a turn shaking and then tossing the dice. The one who gets the highest score (adding the numbers on the dice) is the first player.

NOW the players take turns tossing the dice. If a player does not like the numbers he has tossed, he may have three turns. On the third turn he must take the total number of points shown on the five dice.

THE OBJECT of the game is to reach the highest score with only eleven turns for each player. After tossing the dice, the player marks the number he wants to take from his dice. He does not have to toss the required numbers in order, he adds them to his score paper when he gets them. This is what he is trying to find:

As many #1 dice as possible.
As many #2 dice as possible.
As many #3 dice as possible.   As he writes his
As many #4 dice as possible.   score, he adds
As many #5 dice as possible.   up each of these.
As many #6 dice as possible.

A BIG HOUSE—2 alike
   and 3 alike   (Score 50 for this)
A HIGH HOUSE—2, 3, 4, 5, 6   (Score 50 for this)
A SMALL HOUSE—1, 2, 3, 4, 5   (Score 50 for this)
CHOICE HOUSE—any total the player wants to add
   up in a toss.
YAP—all the numbers alike.   (Score 100 for this)

Battleship
(A game for Father and Son)

MATERIALS: A large sheet of paper and pencil for each player.

DRAW a big square on the paper and mark it off into 100 squares—ten each way. Number the sections on the left

side (from one to ten), and letter the sections at the
top (A through J). The top is North, the bottom South,
the left West, and the right is East. (See illustration.)

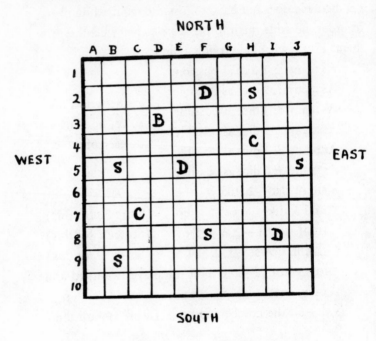

EACH PLAYER has the following fleet of war ships:

1 Battleship
2 Cruisers
3 Destroyers
5 Submarines

TO PLAY the game, each player places his fleet in squares
on his chart, hiding it from the other player. Then, in
turn, the players fire shots at one another. As they do

this, they try to figure out where the other player's ships are located so they can fire at them. If a player thinks the other one knows where he has a ship, he "moves" in his turn instead of firing, unless he thinks he can fire on and sink the ship that is ready to attack him.

RULES AND PLAYS

BATTLESHIP—can move 5 squares in any direction
can fire up to 5 shots at a turn
it takes 5 shots to sink it
CRUISER—can move 3 squares in any direction
can fire up to 3 shots at a turn
it takes 3 shots to sink it
DESTROYER—can move 2 squares in any direction
can fire up to 2 shots at a turn
it takes 2 shots to sink it
SUBMARINE—can move 1 square in any direction
can fire up to 5 shots at a turn
it takes only 1 shot to sink it
("Any direction" means horizontally, vertically, diagonally.)

A PLAYER may either shoot or move in his turn.
If a shot does not hit anything, the other player replies, "Splash."
If a ship has been hit (and the shot has to land in the square where the ship is stationed), it must be marked for each hit, until it is "sunk" by the number of shots that are required to sink it.

A player cannot "move" twice in successive turns.

A COLLISION comes when two ships land in the same square. If you suspect the other player has a ship in the same square as you have one of your ships, tell him, "I think we have a collision." If one of the ships is a submarine, it is sunk. Two submarines on the same square are both sunk. Any ship that is heavier than the other ship it meets in the same square, is wounded, but the other ship is sunk. If both ships are the same kind (but not both submarines), they are only wounded when they meet in the same square—unless they have already been wounded by shots.

THE FIRING is done this way: "I am firing 5 shots, south west into F 4." The enemy knows from that that the ship firing must be a Battleship which is north east of square F 4.

Games to Play on an Auto Trip

(The driver of the car must not take part in these. His attention should be on the road and safe driving.)

WATCH THE NUMBER PLATES:

    See if you can name the capital of each out-of-state . car.

    Keep a list of all the out-of-state cars you see.

WATCH THE CARS YOU SEE:

Make a list of all the ornaments you see on cars.

See if you can name the make of each car.

MAKE A LIST OF VIOLATIONS you see on the road:

Passing on a hill or corner.

Not using signals.

Not stopping for lights.

Neglecting to stop at a stop street.

Speeding.

Driving on the wrong side.

Passing on the right.

Throwing papers, etc., on the road.

Driving without lights or only one light, after dark.

Games to Play in the Car

"I'M GOING TO EUROPE": Each player takes a turn telling how he goes to Europe. He must go on something that will move and it must be seen as he rides in the car. Players drop out of the game when they can not name something new. (Suggestions: bus, plane, boat, floating log, cloud, bird, fly, etc.)

"I'M THINKING OF SOMETHING IN THIS CAR": The leader thinks of something in or on the car. It doesn't have to be seen. Each player has a guess in turn and the answers from the leader can be only "yes" and "no." The person who guesses right is the next leader.

NAMES: The first player names something he sees from the car. The next player must name something he sees but it has to begin with the last letter of the object just named. Example: "Cow" is given. The next player has to give something that begins with a "W," like "Windmill." The name after that might be "Lilac," etc.

"I'M GOING TO A PLACE BEGINNING WITH —": The first player starts with an A. For instance, he might think of "Alabama." The other players try to guess the name of the place. The one who guesses correctly takes the letter B and thinks of a place beginning with that letter. See how long you can keep the game going—through the alphabet as many times as necessary.

CLAP A TUNE and see who can guess it. The answer must be sung.

COUNT THE QUESTIONS: One player thinks of something and the rest of the players are allowed a total of twenty-one questions they may ask to try to guess what it is. The object is to select the questions carefully as the only answer can be "Yes" or "No." The player who guesses correctly has the next turn to think of something. If, however, no one guesses right, the answer is told, and the same player thinks of something new. These are the logical first questions:

"Is it animal?"

"Is it vegetable?"

"Is it mineral?"

ALPHABET FOOD: The leader starts by saying, "When we stop for lunch, I am going to have ...." He names something beginning with the letter A—such as "apple." The next player repeats what the first has said and adds something more to eat—beginning his word with the letter B. (He might say "biscuit.")
The game continues through the alphabet and any player who cannot think of a food with his letter, or misses the list of other foods—which he must repeat in order—must drop out of the game.

When the game progresses, it will go something like this: "When we stop for lunch I am going to have an apple, a biscuit, cake, dates, eggs, fish, grapes, hash, ice cream, junket, kale, lemonade, mashed potato, nuts, onion, plums, quince, rice, stew, turnip—then someone may be stuck to find a food beginning with the letter U. If he is smart, however, he will use an adjective before the food—which is allowed in the game in order to keep it going a long time. He might say, "underfed chicken," "ugly duckling," "unsavory garlic," or "untold pieces of candy." These adjectives will keep the game amusing.

Car Poker

EACH PLAYER takes turns with the cars that pass, using the number plates for poker hands. Here is a list of poker hands as they can be found on the number plates, and they are listed in the order of their value, beginning with the lowest:

    One pair (two numbers alike on one plate)
    Two pair (four numbers alike on one plate)
    Three of a kind (three of the same number)
    Straight (five numbers in numerical order)
    Full House (three of a kind and two of a kind)
    Four of a kind (four of the same number)

IF more than one player has pairs, the highest pair wins. If they have the same numbers, the first wins.

The Game of Ghosts

FINISH THE WORD: The object of this game is for each player to give a letter of the alphabet that will eventually spell a word, but to try not to finish it.

THE FIRST PLAYER starts by saying, "I'm thinking of a

word that begins with the letter——" (Suppose he says "D."

THE NEXT PLAYER adds a letter, as he thinks of a word, but he tries to add something that will not finish a word.

FOR INSTANCE, if he says "DO," he finishes the word; but if he says "D I" the next player is left to add his letter.

EACH PLAYER tries to keep the word going as long as possible, for anyone finishing the word is one-third of a "Ghost," and when he has finished three words, he is out of the game and a full "Ghost."

A GHOST cannot continue to play the game, and if anyone talks to him, he too becomes a ghost. So a ghost tries to make the players speak to him, by asking questions, etc.

A PLAYER may be challenged if he is suspected of adding a letter that will not make a word. If he is caught without a real word, he becomes one-third of a "Ghost."

Party Games

WHO AM I?

THIS game can be played with any number of people.

One player leaves the room and the others decide what
he is to be. (It might be a professional man, the king or
president of some country, an actor, etc.) When he is
called back into the room, the other players, in turn,
make remarks about him, mentioning things that will
give clues to who the character is. From what they say,
he tries to guess who he is supposed to be.

Example: If he is a fisherman, they might say, "He likes
to exaggerate weight." "He's just tied up his boat." or
"Look at the flies he has. They certainly must bite." etc.

NAMES

THIS is a writing game. Paper and pencils are distributed
to each player. A letter of the alphabet is selected, and at
a given signal each one must write all the names he can
think of beginning with that letter. It might be girls'
names, boys' names, cities, towns, or whatever the group
decides. A time limit should be set—say ten minutes.

CONSEQUENCES

EACH player is given a strip of paper and a pencil. He
writes a line on the top of the paper, folds over the writing, and passes it to the person on his left. (He receives
a folded paper from the one on his right.) This continues until the following has been written on each
player's strip of paper:

    A boy's name
    A date
    Where he was

How he looked
How he acted
A girl's name
What she had on
What she said
What they did
The consequences

The Game of Murder
(A party game)

THIS GAME is more fun if it is played by a large group. It requires at least six players.

A DISTRICT ATTORNEY is appointed by the group. He leaves the room while the other players select the Murderer.

ALL LIGHTS in the house are turned out. The District Attorney stays in one spot—where the other players will not mistake him for someone else. All the other players scatter, and continue to move about until the Murderer grabs someone, who screams. When he screams, the Murderer tries to reach a spot where he will not be suspected before the lights are turned on.

WHEN the lights are turned on, everyone gathers in a group around the District Attorney, for him to cross examine, and try to discover who did the murdering. Everyone in the group, except the Attorney, knows who is the Murderer.

THESE RULES are followed in the cross examination: The Victim cannot talk. He is supposed to be dead. The Murderer can lie, except if he is asked, "Did you do it?"

THE DISTRICT ATTORNEY can question the players, but not the Victim, and everyone must tell the truth, except the Murderer. The question, "Did you do it?" can be asked only once.

THE PLAYERS try to make their answers misleading, but they must not lie.

Games for All Ages

Collage Contest

GIVE each person a sheet of construction paper, a pair

of scissors, a piece of string 12″ long, a piece of ribbon 6″ long, 4 toothpicks, and some cellophane tape. Set the kitchen minute timer to ring in 5 minutes and ask the players to make a picture with this collection before the bell rings. (This is a good game for a children's party.)

SPOOL CONTEST

COLLECT a basket of spools and see who can pile the largest number on the palm of his left hand.

A GUESSING GAME

PUT several small articles in a large paper bag. Tie the top together with a string. Now have each player try to guess what is in the bag by feeling of it. (Collect these things for the bag: a small bell, a comb, a spoon, a ball, a pencil, a candle, a glove, shoe horn, a nail, a key, and a bottle cap.

Magic Tricks for Family Fun

THE VANISHING PENNY TRICK is easy to do, but you must be quick about it so that the audience will not see how it is done.

SHOW a penny to your audience and explain that you are going to make it vanish by rubbing it on

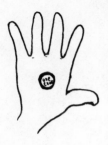

your forearm. Roll up your left sleeve and show that you are holding the penny in your right hand.

WHEN you start rubbing the penny on your arm, suddenly drop it on the floor—pretending it was accidental. Pick it up quickly with your left hand—explaining that you are sorry it slipped. Now continue to rub your arm with the right hand, as if it still held the penny. After a little rubbing, show your empty right hand and say, "See, the penny has disappeared."

WITH THIS CARD TRICK, you will need a helper. It must be someone who knows the trick. But don't let the audience know he is working with you—have him pretend that the trick is new to him.

HOLD UP a pack of cards with the backs toward you, and the faces for the audience to see.

EXPLAIN that you will tell everytime you come to a face card: a Jack, Queen, or King.

SLOWLY lift off each top card, one by one. Pretend you are thinking hard as you do this. Have it planned with someone who knows the trick that when you come to a face card, he will touch some part of his head, to tell you. He must do it so that the audience will not catch on. (Have him rub his eye, play with his hair, or perhaps blow his nose.)

THE MAGIC STAR TRICK

MATERIALS: Five toothpicks
A plate
A few drops of water (in a spoon)

BEND the five toothpicks in half but do not break them. Place them on the plate in the position shown in the illustration. (All the bent centers together.)

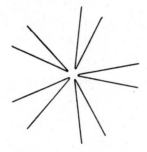

NOW pour a few drops of water over the center of the toothpick design.

WAIT a few minutes, and Magic! The bent toothpicks will move and form a star.

Stunts

CAN YOU DO THESE STUNTS?

PICK UP a pencil with the toes of one foot.

WRITE your name with a pencil held in your teeth.

TIE a knot and bow with one hand.

WRITE your name on a piece of paper held in front of a mirror and looking in the mirror as you do this.

STAND on one foot only and kiss the floor.

DRINK water from the back side of a cup.

 CLASP your hands together in front of you and keep them together while you lift both feet over them.

LIE flat on the floor with your arms crossed over your chest and try to get up without using your hands, arms or elbows.

Chapter 6

Puzzles and Games

to Play Alone

How Many?

HOW MANY WORDS can you find that are pronounced the same but spelt differently? (Example: two, to, too.)

HOW MANY WORDS can you think of that make another word if spelt backward? (Example: dam, mad.)

HOW MANY PIECES of clothing can you name beginning with the letter "S?"

HOW MANY THINGS to eat can you name beginning with the letter "M?"

HOW MANY THINGS can you see from where you are sitting that begin with the letter "P?"

HOW MANY OTHER WORDS can you make by adding letters before or after the following? (Example: take the word RIP and make the words triple, trip, and tripe.)

CAT	HER	IN	ANT	MEN
WE	ON	SIDE	EAR	SO
MAT	HAM	OF	IT	FOR

Scrambles

How quickly can you unscramble these states?

SEHUMATSATCSS
BALAMAA
NEAMI
RIOGGEA
SNATHIONWG
TEVOMRN
SANKSA
NICAGIMH
REALWEAD
VADEAN
YARNDAML
OIOH
INAGRIVI
ETYKCKUN
RANIOZA
DLARIOF
FLORANICAI
NESSETENE
KALASA
GOONER
TONNAMA
AXTES

ANSWERS: Massachusetts, Alabama, Maine, Georgia, Washington, Vermont, Kansas, Michigan, Delaware, Nevada, Maryland, Ohio, Virginia, Kentucky, Arizona, Florida, California, Tennessee, Alaska, Oregon, Montana, Texas.

The Animal Fair Scramble

Unscramble these animals that went to the fair:

NDKEOY

NLPAEEHT

GITRE

RAGIFEF

NOIL

BERZA

SERHO

ELSA

RABE

CLAME

DAPEROL

NOPY

TOGA

LUME

GOANKARO

ANSWERS: donkey, elephant, tiger, giraffe, lion, zebra, horse, seal, bear, camel, leopard, pony, goat, mule, kangaroo.

A Scavenger Hunt

Take a small basket or box and see how quickly you can find these things in your house. (If you have a brother or sister to do it too, see who gets them all first.)

Safety pin
Eraser
Rubber band
Bobby pin
Pencil
Feather
Toothpick
Shoe lace
Used postage stamp
Paper clip
Piece of string
Eraser
Comb
Penny
Button
Tape measure
Nail
Bottle cap

How Many Words?

Using any of the letters in each word how many words
can you find in each one of the following?

DICTIONARY
ALPHABET
BIRTHDAY
CONSTRUCTION
DEMOCRATIC

TRESPASSING
SCHOLARSHIP
MINISTER
PHYSICIAN

Scrambled Flowers

Can you unscramble these flowers?

SAYID
LEOTIV
SNAPY
SORE
PLUIT
SUCCOR
YILL
DARMGILO
NIZIAN
VELORC
SRATE
KNIP
PYOPP
YOLLH
CHIORD
TEPUIAN

ANSWERS: daisy, violet, pansy, rose, tulip, crocus, lily, marigold, zinnia, clover, aster, pink, poppy, holly, or-chid, petunia.

Rhyme the Name

Each of the words listed below rhymes with a boy's or girl's name. Can you rhyme the name? (Example: CANE—JANE.)

BOYS	GIRLS
BACK	BANNER
MUD	NOSE
PILL	MOAN
HEN	CINDER
PICK	BASE
SNARL	PAN
METER	METER
HOBBY	SPOT
BIKE	BADGE
HOE	MEAN
HAM	FANCY
NEW	TABLE
STEAL	JUICY
BALL	LEG
DIM	TALLY
TANK	GLUE
MERRY	LATE
HAT	FACE

ANSWERS: BOYS: Jack, Bud, Bill, Ben, Dick, Carl, Peter, Bobby, Mike, Joe, Sam, Hugh, Neal, Paul, Tim, Frank, Jerry, Pat. GIRLS: Anna, Rose, Joan, Linda, Grace, Ann, Rita, Dot, Madge, Jean, Nancy, Mable, Lucy, Peg, Sally, Sue, Kate, Grace.

Can You Read These Words?

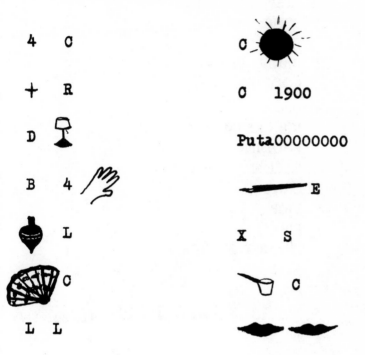

ANSWERS: foresee, adder, delight, beforehand, topple, fancy, tools, season, sedate, potatoes, penny, excess, pansy, tulips.

What Letter Is It?

What letter can you find in:
    SPAGHETTI
    HASH

CHEESE
STEW
SOUP
PEAS
BAKED BEANS
COOKIES

But not in:

ICE CREAM
PUDDING
BACON
CAKE
RICE
PIE
PEANUT BUTTER
JAM

ANSWER: The 19th letter in the alphabet.

Cut and Fit

WITH a sheet of tracing paper make a copy of each of these odd shaped pieces, cut them out and fit them together to make something that rhymes with SPARE.

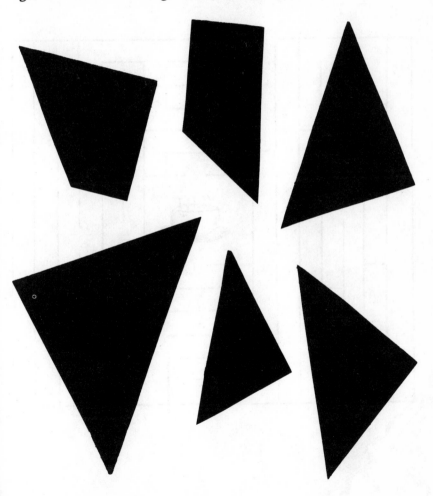

Find the Cake

SOMEONE is having a birthday. Can you find your way to the birthday cake starting on the outside of the field and not jumping over any wall?

Find the Road That Leads to the Runaway Horse

Mrs. Brown Does Her Errands

MRS. BROWN has several errands to do before she picks up the children at school. Find the way she went to do everything on her list and not go over the same road twice.

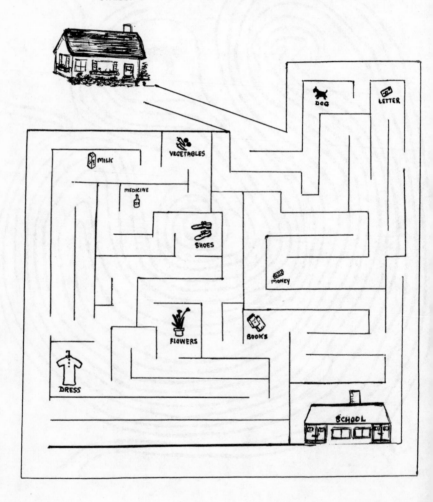

MRS. BROWN'S LISTS:

> Buy vegetables at the market
> Pick up dress at the cleaner's
> Collect books at the library
> Get shoes at the cobbler's
> Buy milk at the dairy
> Mail a letter at the Post Office
> Buy flowers at the florist's
> Pick up a bottle of medicine at the drug store
> Get some money at the bank
> Take the dog to the kennel

Chapter 7

Indoor Work Shop

Carpentry

Shoe Shine Stool

MATERIALS: ¾″ lumber

Saws—cross cut and coping

2 butt hinges, (2″ length)

A hammer and nails

A welding rod (which can be bought at a garage)

4 screw eyes

Wire cutters or a cold chisel

Sandpaper

THE STOOL can be finished with varnish or stain, or painted to match the color scheme of the room.

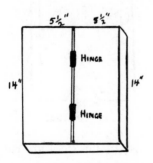

THE TOP of the stool is made in two pieces, 5½″ by 14″ each. These are hinged together on the long edge, so one half can be folded back on top of the other half.

When they are folded this way, the top will be a shoe shine foot rest, and through the opening will be a shelf to store polishing materials. When you have sawed the two top pieces the correct size, sand the rough edges before putting on hinges.

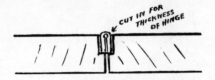

THE HINGES are screwed to a long edge of each top piece, about 1″ from the corner. First cut a groove in the edge, making it the thickness of the hinge. This will make the hinge fit into the wood and prevent too much of a crack in the top when the two pieces are hinged together and form the top of the stool.

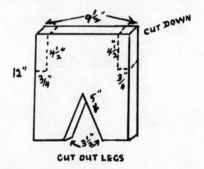

CUT OUT LEGS

THE TWO LEG SIDES of the stool are cut as illustrated: 12″ high and 9½″ wide. Saw a triangular piece from the bottom edge of each piece. Draw the triangle first, having the bottom 3½″ and the point 5″ from the base. On the top edge of the leg piece, cut out a section at each corner, where the side pieces can be fitted. (See illustration.) These should be ¾″ deep—or the thickness of the wood, and 4½″ long.

A BOTTOM SECTION should be cut to fit inside the legs, between the side pieces. This will be the bottom of the box to hold polishing materials. Saw this piece 8″ wide and 10½″ long.

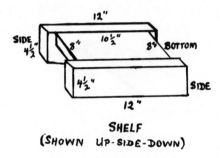

SHELF
(SHOWN UP-SIDE-DOWN)

THE TWO SIDES should be cut 12″ long and 4½″ wide.

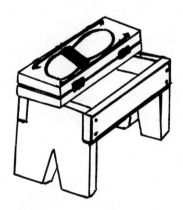

THE FOOT REST, which is mounted on the inside of the hinged top, can either be cut with a coping saw from ply wood (trace a man size shoe for a pattern), or you can buy a cheap pair of wood sandals, remove the straps, and use one of the soles for mounting.

THE WELDING ROD is used to hold the polishing cloth as it is being pulled from side to side over the shoe. Cut the rod in half—with wire cutters or a cold chisel. Fasten one of the rods on each side of the foot rest, by running each end through a screw eye and bending the end back to hold it.

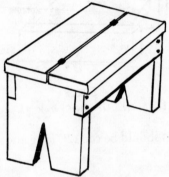

TO PUT THE STOOL TOGETHER, work in this order: First finish the top, put on hinges, foot rest, and rod holders. Next fit the bottom shelf to the two side rails, centering it so the four ends are left ready to be fitted into the leg grooves and it is even with the bottom edge of each side rail. Nail or glue it in place.

NOW fit the legs to the bottom, with the four side rail ends resting in the corner grooves. Nail the side rails to the legs.

LAST of all fit on the top. Nail down the half that is to be stationary.

SANDPAPER all the rough edges and then paint or varnish the stool.

A Raised Cutting Board

THIS cutting board is made so a dish may be slipped under it to catch the food as it is sliced.

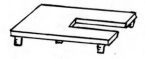

MATERIALS: A piece of plywood 10″ by 12″ and ½″ thick

Five empty wooden sewing thread spools or a ¾″ dowl stick 6¼″ long (for legs)

A coping saw

Household cement

Sandpaper

IN THE MIDDLE of one of the 10″ sides of the plywood mark off a 6″ square section (leaving 2″ on each side of it). Saw out this square with a coping saw. .

SANDPAPER all the edges of the board, and around the square opening.

IF you are using a dowl stick for legs, saw it into five pieces of equal length (1¼″ each). Sandpaper the legs so they are smooth.

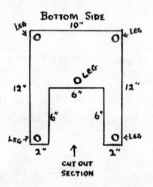

CEMENT the legs to the bottom of the board at each outside corner. Fasten the fifth leg about an inch from the middle of the inside edge of the opening. (See illustration.)

Children's Blocks

WHEN you want a set of blocks for children, ask a local carpenter or cabinet maker if you can have his scraps of wood. They can be sanded into beautiful blocks. The

odd shapes will fascinate children and make them better
than many expensive sets.

A Rustic Bird House

MATERIALS: Slabs of wood (with the bark on)
A saw
Nails
A screw eye

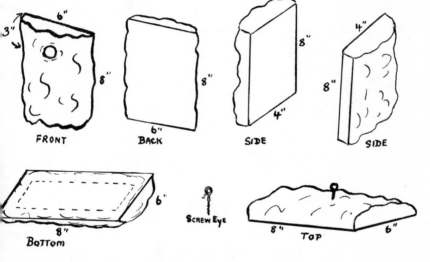

FRONT   BACK   SIDE   SIDE

SCREW EYE   BOTTOM   TOP

SAW the slabs into these pieces (see illustration):
2 pieces 8″ by 6″—the top and bottom
2 pieces 8″ by 6″—the front and back
2 pieces 8″ by 4″—the sides

CUT the round hole on the front piece about three inches from the top. The size will depend on what bird you want to attract to the house. Plan it for the kind you have seen in the neighborhood. Here are a few names and the size entrance hole each bird will want:

Bluebird, wren, and tree swallow—1½"
Chickadee and nut hatch—1¼"
Downy woodpecker and fly catcher—2"

IF you have a hole-saw, cut the opening entrance with that. Another way to do it is with a coping saw. First mark the hole on the inside, then with a rip saw split the front in half through the middle. Saw the hole on each piece of wood, and then glue the two pieces back together.

NAIL all the pieces together (as illustrated) after the hole has been cut.

An Extra Counter

IF you need more counter space in your kitchen, on your porch, or in a study, hinge a piece of plywood, (a pastry or large cutting board can be used) to a wall or door. Use a narrow board for a hinged leg, which can be raised to hold up the counter.

MATERIALS: A board 24½″ by 17½″ and ¾″ thick
            Another board 22″ by 1½″ and ¾″ thick
            A hook and eye—the hook 1½″ long
            3 butt hinges 3″ by 3″ (open)
            Screws
            A saw
            Sandpaper

FIRST saw your board and leg to the measurements given.
Sand the edges smooth, being especially careful to sand
the outside corners so they will not be sharp.

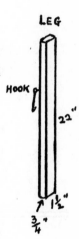

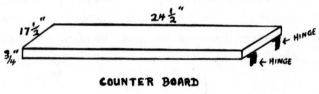

COUNTER BOARD

FASTEN two hinges to the bottom inside edge of the
counter board, spacing them the same distance from each
side.

FASTEN the third hinge to the bottom inside edge of the
leg piece.

MARK on the wall where the counter is to go, and the
height you want the counter. Measure 5¼″ below this
and screw in the eye (on the middle of the wall) at this
level. Measure 3¼″ below this and make a mark. This

will be where the joint of the leg hinge will go. Now fasten the other half of the leg hinge to the wall.

NEXT fasten the two counter hinges to the wall, above the leg and where you marked the height. Be sure the middle of the inside edge is directly over the leg.

LIFT the counter so it is at a right-angle with the wall, and raise the leg so it touches the bottom side of the counter. Hold your hook, fastened through the eye on the wall, and stretch it to the raised leg—to see where it should be attached in order to hold the leg up and keep the counter level. (You will need someone to help you because you will want a free hand to mark where to screw in the hook.)

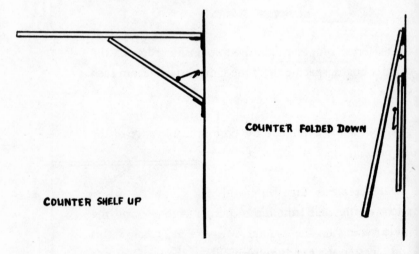

COUNTER FOLDED DOWN

COUNTER SHELF UP

IF you are painting or staining the counter, do this before you hinge it to the wall.

Bird Feeding Station

MATERIALS: The best wood to use for this is a slab sawed from a tree log, with the bark left on. This is to attract even the most timid birds by using natural materials. One side will be flat and the outside will be rounded. If you live in the country, you can pick up slabs at a saw mill. You will need for carpentry tools: a saw, hammer, some nails, and a large 2″ screw-eye.

SAW the wood slab to make the following pieces:
   1 piece 8″ by 12″ (for the bottom)
   2 pieces 6″ by 5″ (for the ends)
   1 piece 10″ by 5″ (for the back)
   1 piece 6″ by 12″ (for the roof top)

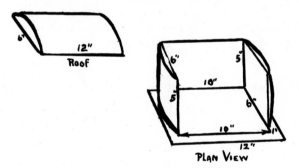

NAIL the pieces together in this order: (Make sure to drive in the nails from the bark side, leaving the smooth side inside.)

   Fasten the 2 ends to the back.

   Fasten these three pieces toward the rear of the bottom platform as shown in the illustration, to allow a landing ledge for the birds at the front opening.

NAIL the top on and install a large size screw-eye in balance point.

A Desk Letter Rack

MATERIALS: 2 wire coat-hangers and a block of wood about 7″ long, 5″ wide, and 1″ thick.

CARPENTRY tools you will need are: a plane, a wire cutter, a saw, sandpaper, and ⅛″ hand drill, ruler and a pencil.

PAINT or stain can be used to finish the rack.

FIRST saw the wood the size needed.

PLANE the two long edges, to round them.

SANDPAPER the block until it is smooth.

NOW mark dots on the top of the block—to show where you will need to make holes. These holes will be along the long edges—about ½″ from the side. The first one should be ⅞″ from the end, and the next three 1¾″ apart. (See the illustration.)

THE HOLES are drilled about ½″ deep. If you do not have a drill, pound in nails, then remove them. The holes must slope to agree with the wire angles.

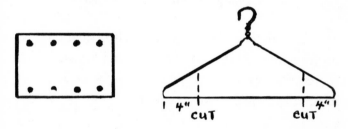

CUT OFF the rounded ends of two coat hangers 4″ from the end. (Measure the straight side, and cut the curved side in line with this. See illustration.)

NOW push the two ends of each wire into the two opposite holes along the sides of the block.

FINISH the rack with bright enamel paint or, if you prefer, stain the wood.

THIS RACK can be used to hold letters, paper, small books, and pamphlets.

A Child's Sandbox on Wheels

THIS sandbox is made so it can be rolled from one end of the yard to another, to move it in and out of the sun as desired. This way the child can be in the shade on hot days, and play in the sun on cool days.

MATERIALS: For the bottom: ⅛″ Masonite, or ¼″ exterior plywood, 42″ by 60″

For sides: 2″ by 4″ measuring 56¾″ (2 pieces)

For ends: 2″ by 4″ measuring 42″ (pieces)

Four seats to be made from a ¾″ board 8″ wide and 42″ long. The seats will be 11″ by 11″ by 15½″, sawed into a triangular shape. (See illustration.)

The wheels: 4 typical garden wheelbarrow rubber-tired replacement wheels 6″ or 8″ in size.

Axle stock: 2 pieces ½″ diameter and about 48″ long. (Each axle should be

42" long plus twice the hub length of
whatever wheels are used, plus 1".)

Hardware: No. 6 or No. 8 galvanized
nails; No. 10 galvanized screws 1¼"
long; eight No. 8 galvanized round head
screws 1" long; galvanized flat head
wood-screws 1½" long; four ½" steel
straps (clamps) as used for pipe or con-
duit installation, and four ⅛" diameter
cotter pins.

Carpentry tools: hammer, screwdriver,
plane, saw, drill and counter-sink, and a
drill press or electric drill. (The wheels
and axle stock can be bought through
one of the mail order catalogs.)

THE ILLUSTRATION is an "exploded" view. Follow this
in planning and sawing the sandbox. The four seats are
gussets nailed to the top to hold the "2 by 4s" together.
The plywood bottom should be screwed to the side and
end pieces. Space the screws about 8" apart.

If the seat gusset material selected is one which splits
easily, it will be better to drill and countersink and attach the gusset by No. 10 by 1½" galvanized flat head
woodscrews, spaced approximately 4" apart.

THE AXLES are installed by turning the box up-side-down
and laying them across each end, spaced about 2½" back
from the box ends. Now drop the four steel straps over
the axles and in such a location as will allow the eight

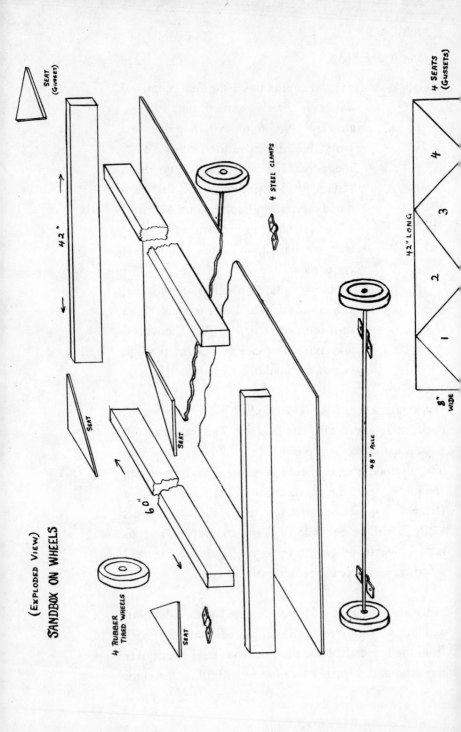

(EXPLODED VIEW)
SANDBOX ON WHEELS

SEAT (GUSSET)

42"

SEAT

6"

4 RUBBER TIRED WHEELS

SEAT

SEAT

4 STEEL CLAMPS

48" AXLE

4 SEATS (GUSSETS)

42" LONG

1 2 3 4

8" WIDE

attaching screws to go through the box floor and directly into the "2 by 4s".

THE WHEELS are to be installed after the axles are in place. First slip all four wheels onto the four axle ends, and mark the four axles for drilling, just at the outer hub edge of each wheel. Then remove the wheels and axles and drill through the latter for $\frac{1}{8}''$ cotter pins.

FOR A FINISH—First sand the rough edges, then paint the box with a pleasing shade of green house paint. It should have two coats of paint.

Chapter 8

Costumes for Holiday Parades and Parties

Costume Make-Up

THE products listed below may be purchased at a drug store where they sell make-up.

NOSE PUTTY can be molded to change the contours of a face, to make a devil's chin, a clown's big nose, etc.

SPIRIT GUM is used to stick on a mustache, eyebrows, and such; but chewing gum can be used.

CREPE HAIR is used by theatre people, but fringed crepe paper can also be used.

CLOWN WHITE can be used with rouge in making up a clown.

SILVER DUST SPRAY or talcum powder will make white hair for your costume.

AN EYE-BROW PENCIL helps to make up an elderly character. Follow the person's own lines to make the shadows and wrinkles look real. Have him smile, frown, etc., to show his true lines. Also make dark shadows under the eyes.

A Nurse's Uniform

MATERIALS: A man's plain white handkerchief
An old sheet and some blue dye to color it
A large dress snap
String
A pencil
Scissors
Needle and thread
White shoes
A white dress—skirt or petticoat

FOR THE CAPE you need a wide piece of material. An old sheet, dyed blue, works beautifully. The cape is cut in a half circle. Make a newspaper pattern before you cut the cloth. You will need to pin two or three pages of the paper together to make it the desired width.

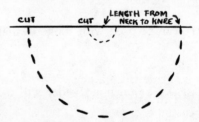

MEASURE the distance from your neck to your knees, and draw a half circle this width on the paper. Tie a string to a pencil or crayon. Hold the end of the string down on the edge of the paper with one hand, and with the other hand holding the pencil, stretch the string so you can draw a half circle on the paper from the edge around to the edge again. In the middle of the straight edge on your pattern, draw another half circle, using a 6″ length of string. (This half circle will be the neck opening on your cape.)

SEW a narrow hem around the entire edge of the cape to finish it. Then sew a snap to the two corners at the neck opening.

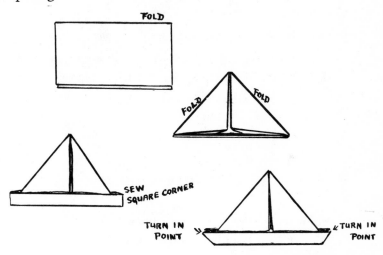

THE CAP can be made from a man's handkerchief. Fold the handkerchief in half, then fold the two top corners on the folded edge down to the middle of the bottom edge. Turn up three thicknesses at the bottom edge about 2″. Turn the cap over and fold up the single bottom edge the same distance. Slip the two side points, at the bottom, inside the front band, to make square corners. Sew these folds to hold them together. Also sew down the band at the middle of the front, to hold the center folds together.

Be careful not to sew through to the back of the cap. When the band of the cap has been fastened securely, hold the middle of the front edge with one hand, and the middle of the back edge with the other hand, separating the two edges. Now fold the cap through the middle of the front and the middle of the back, so it makes a bonnet. Sew the front and bottom bands together at the lower corners on both sides of the cap.

THE NURSE'S CAPE AND CAP should be worn with a white dress and shoes. If you haven't a white dress, a white skirt or plain white petticoat and white blouse will do.

A Brownie Costume

MATERIALS: This costume is made with a blouse top, to be worn with brown shorts or pedal pushers. The material for the blouse should match the color of the shorts. You will also need one dozen or more tiny bells, scissors, needle, thread, and dress snaps.

CUT a pattern from newspaper first, following the diagram illustrated.

SEW UP the side seams on the wrong side. Turn under the edge at the bottom of each sleeve (about ¼″), and hem. Make the same width hem on both sides of the front opening and around the bottom of the blouse.

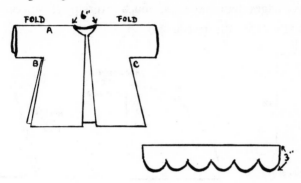

CUT two strips of cloth 3″ wide and about 18″ long, and another strip 3″ wide and about 40″ long (the length depending on the size of the blouse). Fringe or scallop the edge of each strip.

GATHER the two 18″ fringed strips and sew them to the bottom of the jacket sleeves. Gather the long fringed strip and sew it around the neck of the blouse.

SEW on snaps to fasten the front of the jacket, and sew tiny bells to the fringe around the neck.

FOR THE CAP, cut a newspaper pattern of an 18″ quarter circle. Cut it from the corner of the paper, having the two sides 18″ long, and round the edge opposite the corner. A good way to do this is to tie an 18″ string to a pencil. Hold the end of the string at the corner, and draw with the pencil, stretching the string as far as it will go.

WHEN you have cut the newspaper pattern, roll it into a cap and try it on for fit. You may find it too big, so the two edges will have too much overlap. If so, cut it smaller. (See illustration.)

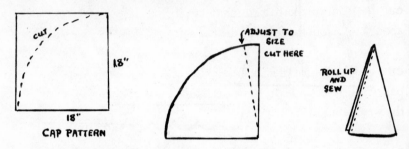

CAP PATTERN

CUT the cloth to fit the pattern, then sew up the seam of the cap on the wrong side (with the two straight edges together). Turn the cap right side out and sew a bell to the point at the top of the cap.

HEM or make tiny scallops on the bottom edge of the cap.

Space Man Costume

MATERIALS: A large paper bag
A sheet of transparent paper (cellophane)
Heavy aluminum foil
Paper fasteners
Scissors

THE SPACE HELMET

CUT OFF the top of the bag so it is the right size to fit over your head and pull down to your shoulders. Then cut out the front of the bag to make an oblong opening— about 1½″ from the folds of the bag.

CUT a window for this opening, from the transparent paper. Make it at least 1″ wider than the opening, all the way around.

FASTEN the window to the bag with paper fasteners, spacing them at equal distances all the way around the window.

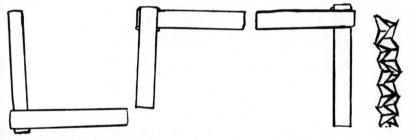

ANTENNAE can be made for the space helmet by cutting the heavy aluminum foil into 1″ strips and folding two strips together the following way: Lay one strip on the table, straight up and down in front of you. Then place the end of another strip across the bottom end of the first piece of foil. (See illustration.) Fold the first strip down over the second, then fold the second across the first, fold up the first over the second and continue to fold this way until the two strips are completely folded, one on top of the other.

FASTEN one folded end of the antenna to the top of the paper helmet, using a paper fastener.

ADD as many antennae to your helmet as you like.

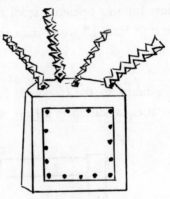

A Pirate Costume

MATERIALS: An old pair of dungarees
A striped T shirt
2 bandannas
2 brass curtain rings
2 paper clips

CUT OFF the legs of the dungarees, just below the knees,

and fringe the edge by cutting three-inch deep points all around.

TIE one bandanna around your waist and knot it at the hip.

TIE the other bandanna around your head and knot it over one ear.

USE the two curtain rings for ear rings, and fasten them through the paper clips so each clip can slip over the lobe of your ear.

Quick Costumes to Assemble

TRAMP

MATERIALS: An old torn hat, dungarees with odd colored patches glued or basted on the back and front, an old shirt with one torn sleeve and the other sleeve missing, old shoes, and a stick with a bandanna—filled with rolled up paper—tied to it. Black smudges on the face will make you look more like a tramp.

GYPSY

MATERALS: a long full skirt, white full sleeved blouse,

and a kerchief for the head. Wear all the costume
jewelry you can find: earrings, several strings of long
beads, and many bracelets.

SCARECROW

MATERIALS: an old long coat, an old hat (the bigger the
better), and a broom handle or long stick. Do not put
your arms through the coat sleeve but run the stick
through them.

A Witch Costume for Halloween

MATERIALS: 1½ yards black cotton cloth a yard wide
                       Black thread
                       A needle
                       Scissors
                       Newspaper

CUT OFF a yard of the cloth for the cape. The other half-
yard is for a witch hat.

TO MAKE THE CAPE, fold the yard piece of cloth in half,
(with the two cut edges together.) Then fold it in half
again—making a square of the material. Now cut a neck
hole at the folded corner of the cloth, making the hole
the shape of a quarter circle (cutting about three inches

from the corner point.) Cut off the opposite corner of the folded material, from top corner to opposite bottom corner—rounding the edge. (See illustration.) Open the cloth and cut an opening along one of the folds, from the neck opening to the bottom edge. Try on the cape and see if the neck hole is big enough to reach around your neck. If not, fold the cloth again and cut the opening a little larger.

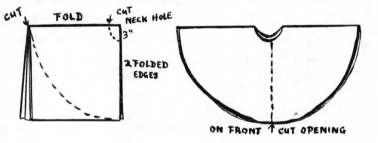

TO MAKE THE HAT, first cut the newspaper. Use a full sheet (four pages). Fold the paper in half, then in half again. With the paper in front of you and the last folded edge at the top and the double folded edge at the left, cut the paper as illustrated—in a straight line from the middle of the two folded edges on the left, to the middle of the bottom open edge.

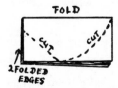

Then make a rounded cut from the outside corner of the top folded edge to the same point on the bottom edge.

SEW
TO CLOTH

ROLL INTO SHAPE

OPEN the last fold of the paper, so it is just two thicknesses, and lay this folded piece on the half yard of material. Pin the newspaper to the cloth and cut around the paper so the cloth is the same size.

WITH your needle and thread, sew close to the edge, fastening the cloth to the paper.

SHAPE the hat by bringing the two short sides together—with the cloth on the outside. Slide one edge over the other until you have a pointed witch hat. Sew the hat so it will stay together in this shape.

A Pilgrim Cape and Bonnet for Thanksgiving

MATERIALS: 1½ yards brown or gray cotton cloth
             Thread to match
             A needle
             Scissors
             Two large white handkerchiefs (the man's size)

FOLD the cloth in half, with the cut edges together. Fold the material again the other way. (Sides together.)

CUT a quarter circle (about three inches wide) at the

folded corner, and round off the opposite corner on the
same folded edge. Open the last fold of the cloth and
cut an opening from the neck hole down the front to the
bottom edge.

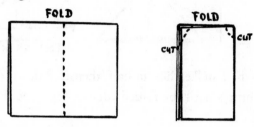

SEW the back and front together from the top fold to the
bottom on each side. Have the cape folded wrong-side
out when you sew.

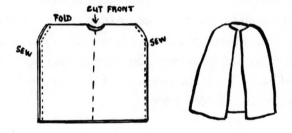

TURN the cape right-side out and sew a double thread,
close to the edge, all around the neck opening. Try on
the cape and pull the thread up so that the neck opening
fits. Knot the thread so the neck of the cape will stay
gathered to the right size.

FOLD one of the large handkerchiefs diagonally and use
this for the collar of the cape.

THE PILGRIM BONNET is made from the other large hand-kerchief.

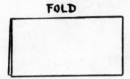  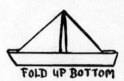

FOLD the handkerchief in half, then fold down the two top corners until the folded edges meet. (See the illustration.)

TURN up the front bottom edge, and at the back, turn up the bottom edge.

BRING the inside of the two bottom corners together and fold the cloth so that the turned-up front edge forms the front of the bonnet, and the turned-up back edge makes the neck band of the bonnet. (See illustration.) Sew the turned-back edge at the two sides of the front to hold the bonnet in its folded shape.

An Indian Hat

MATERIALS: Stiff white paper 9″ by 12″
Crayons
Scissors
Needle and thread

CUT the two pieces of paper into strips, cutting across the paper the narrow way. Make the strips the width you would like to have your feathers.

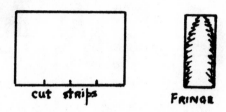

cut strips   FRINGE

COLOR each strip on both sides, using either crayons or paints. These will be your feathers, so after they are colored, fringe the edges to make them look like feathers. Give them a pointed top.

CUT another sheet of paper in half, this time the long way.

cut   SEW

SEW these two pieces of paper together by having two narrow ends overlap. This will make a long strip and it will be the band to hold the feathers.

NOW sew the bottom of each feather to one side of the band.

WHEN the feathers are all fastened to the band, put it around your head and hold the two ends together where

they meet. Take off the hat—still holding the ends—and
sew the band to fasten the ends.

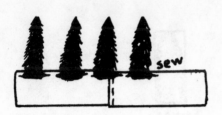  

The Children's Parade

FOR THE children's parade on the Fourth of July, have it
understood that the costumes must all be made from
paper bags. Other materials may be added to give detail,
but the basis of the costume must be paper bags. Here
are some ideas of how the bags may be used:

A GLAMOUR GIRL HEAD can be made from a medium
sized bag. Cut out the lower half of the eye holes, and
fringe the cut piece. Turn it up to look like eye lashes.

(If you want dark lashes, crayon the piece before you fringe it.) Crayon under the opening for the lower lashes, and draw lines for the eye brows. Crayon a bright red heart-shaped mouth. Sew on loops of red yarn for hair, and pin on earrings—the bigger the better.

A HULA HULA SKIRT can be made by cutting several large paper bags into strips and sewing them together, leaving a band at the top to go around the waist. Cut and color several circles of paper. Fringe the edge of each one and sew a string of green yarn through the middle to make a chain that will look like flowers. Make one to wear around your neck, and one for each wrist.

Chapter 9

Weather Forecasting

Will It Be Picnic and Holiday Weather?

THE meteorologist relies on the barometer, thermometer, wind speed indicator and weather vane when he forecasts weather. There are many signs that point to weather changes.

LOOK FOR THESE SIGNS

CLOUDS: If they are low in the sky, it will probably rain. High clouds are not rain clouds.

DEW: Dew on the grass means fair weather. Watch for it either at night or in the early morning.

THE SKY: Mackerel sky (small broken clouds looking like fish scales) and mare's tails (trails of soft thin clouds) mean rain the next day.
Red sky in the morning usually means rain or snow; but when the sky is red at night it means the opposite, that tomorrow will be a nice day.

WIND—IN THE EASTERN PART OF THE COUNTRY: A Southwest storm is usually a quick or short storm, lasting not more than twelve hours, on the average.
West and Northwest wind usually means fair weather.

A Northeast storm can be, and often is, from two to four days in length. So once the wind gets in the east, you had better postpone outdoor activities.

SOUNDS: When there is moisture in the air, sounds carry better. On a dry day sounds are not as clear.

WEATHER TRAVELS from the West to the East, so look to the West for signs of a change.

IN TIME OF DROUGHT all signs fail.

ANIMALS TELL

Birds fly high in fair weather. If they are flying low or stay in the trees, it may mean a storm is coming. Cows tend to lie down in the fields when a storm is coming.
The ground spider's web, seen on the grass in the early morning, indicates a fair day, although it may look threatening.

A RAINBOW

If there is a rainbow in the morning, it usually means more rain coming.

THE SUN AND MOON

A red sun at night usually means a pleasant day to follow. A halo, or ring around the sun or moon, means rain.

TREES

Watch the leaves on the trees. They turn "inside out" (so the back side of the leaf shows) before a storm.

THE BAROMETER

Rising, it means fair weather.
Dropping, expect a storm.
Holding steady, there will probably be no change.

AFTER A STORM, if the moisture or raindrops continue to cling to the trees and windows, it means the rain is not over. When the weather changes, these bits of moisture soon disappear.

How to Keep a Weather Chart

MATERIALS: A large sheet of paper
A ruler
A pencil—or pen and ink

DRAW lines on the sheet of paper to make a column for each day in the month.

CROSS these lines, marking the paper into small squares.

ACROSS the top, write the numbers for the days of the month. Down the left side of the paper put the same numbers you have on your outdoor thermometer.

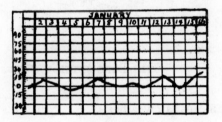

EACH DAY record what your thermometer says, marking it on this chart.

IF you want to add what kind of day it is, use your crayons and color the square each day—use yellow for a sunny day, black dots for rain, light gray for a cloudy day, and draw snowflake dots for a snowstorm.

Why the Weather Changes

1. Our weather is created by the uneven heating of the earth's surface.

2. This therefore leads to the formation of large masses of either cold air or warm air, depending on the point of origin.

3. These large air masses, in contention with each other, generate fair weather, storms, winds, atmospheric pressure, pressure differences (lows and highs), humidity changes, and all of the many factors which go to make up what we know as weather systems.

4. Confining ourselves to the northern half of the western hemisphere, we see these air masses of polar and tropic origins endeavoring to force themselves southward and northward respectively, and finding themselves on a common battleground of our North American land masses.

5. A further great influence on their movement is the rotation of the earth, and the inertia effect of the atmospheric blanket, which imparts a general easterly movement to these great weather systems.

6. A meeting of these air masses—or a line of contact between them—is known as a front (cold or warm, etc.) or frontal system.

7. The lows, or storm areas, are associated with and situated near, the frontal systems.

8. The highs, or fair weather areas, represent the centers or main body of the respective air masses.

9. Cold air masses consist of relatively dry air; warm air masses usually are of moist air (the meteorological law states that the ability of air to hold moisture—that is, the humidity of the air—is in direct ratio to its temperature. So a cubic yard of air at 80° may contain 1 oz.

of water; while a cubic yard of air at 32° may contain
only 1/6 oz. of water, maximum).

10. Thus, if a warm air mass containing nearly saturated
air—that is, relatively high humidity—is being over-run,
or under-wedged, by a cold air mass, the resultant cool-
ing of the warm air will, at that area of contact, bring
about a lowered temperature. At this new temperature,
there is more moisture present than air at that new temperature can retain in suspension. Accordingly, precipitation must occur in one of its well known forms: rain,
snow, cloud, fog, dew, etc.

11. In order to create more effective areas of contact,
and thus increase the extent of precipitation, nature has
provided moving air—that is, wind—by means of a system of pressure differences in the atmosphere. As water
will flow from a higher to a lower level, and electricity
from a positive to a negative pole, so will air move from
a mass at high (or relatively higher) atmospheric pressure, toward an area of low pressure.

Old Sayings About the Weather

"Sunset red and sunrise gray,
   Set the traveler on his way."

"Sunset gray and sunrise red,
   Brings down showers on his head."

"Cobwebs are upon the grass,
  Rain will never come to pass."

"Red sky in the morning,
  Sailors take warning.
  But red sky at night,
  A sailor's delight."

"When the days begin to lengthen,
  Then the winter begins to strengthen."

"If March comes in like a lion,
  It goes out like a lamb."

Weather Superstitions

THE DATE of the first snowstorm predicts the number of storms for the winter. For instance, if the first snow falls on November 26th, there will be 26 snowstorms.

FEBRUARY 2ND is GROUND HOG DAY. If it is sunny so the ground hog sees his shadow, he will go back into his hole and there will be six more weeks of winter.

JULY 15TH is ST. SWITHIN DAY. If it rains on that day, it will continue to rain for 40 days.

WHEN the soot at the back of the fireplace burns, it is going to rain.

WHEN the sky is a soft yellow at sunset, it usually means that rain is coming.

SEE a halo around the sun and look for rain.

TO FARMERS in the north, a red moon means snow is coming.

A PIG running with a straw held in his mouth indicates a big wind is coming.

WHEN the rooster crows in the morning, it means there will be a change in the weather.

IT WILL BE A HARD WINTER IF:
     The caterpillar's coat is unusually thick.

Acorns have big caps.

Pine trees shed many needles.

Crickets come into the house in mid-summer.

Squirrels and chipmunks carry their tails curled high.

Addresses for Handicraft Materials

AMERICAN HANDICRAFTS COMPANY, 1011 Foch Street,
Fort Worth 7, Texas

ARTEX SALES COMPANY, Box 917, Lima, Ohio

BAIM'S INC., 235 South Wabash Avenue, Chicago 4,
Illinois

BOYCAN'S FLORAL ARTS, State and Flower Avenue,
Sharon, Pennsylvania

FLOWERCRAFT SUPPLY COMPANY, P. O. Box 3862,
Seattle 24, Washington

GAGER'S HANDICRAFTS, 1024 Nicollet Avenue, Minneapolis 3, Minnesota

HOLIDAY HANDICRAFTS INC., Apple Hill, Winsted,
Connecticut

KIT KRAFT, 12109 Ventura Place, Studio City, California

LEE WARDS, 615 Page Avenue, Elgin, Illinois

THE O. P. CRAFT COMPANY, INC., Sandusky, Ohio

VANITY FAIR CRAFTS, 1049 North Paulina, Chicago 22,
Illinois

Index

A

Alphabet Food (Game), 179
Amateur Show, 96
Angel for Christmas, 45-47
Animal Crackers, 74
Animal Fair Scramble, 195
Animals
  made from envelopes,
    125-126
  in weather forecasting, 250
Appliqués, 142-144
April Fool's Day, 9-12
  jokes, 11-12
  tricks, 9-11
Aprons
  appliquéed, 143
  Christmas, 54-55
Art, Seaside, 101
Aspic Salad, 8
Aunts, Presents for, 3-6, 56-57
Automobile Games, 176-181

B

Back-Side-To Party, 82
Back To Back Race, 92
Ball of Greens for Christmas,
  51-52
Balloon Party, 74-76
  decorations, 76
  games, 75-76
  invitations, 74-75
Balls for Christmas Tree,
  47-48
Barometers, 251
Baseball, Scrub, 87-89
Baskets, May Day, 16-18
Battleship (Game), 173-176

Beach Activities, 99-102
Bead Doll Book Mark,
  139-140
Bead Star for Christmas Trees,
  50-51
Bean Race, 35-36
Bed Tray Occupations,
  118-119
Bedspread, Doll, 132-134
Beverage Opener, Jewel
    Trimmed, 25
Bird Feeding Station, 219-220
Bird House, 215-216
Bird's Nest, Golden, 48
Birthdays
  cards, 162
  party treasure hunt, 79-81
  presents, 23-24
Blanket from Hand Woven
    Material, 138
Blocks for Children, 214-215
Blotters, 3-4
Boats, Making a Motor for,
  129
Book Marks, 3
  bead doll, 139-140
  on greeting cards, 161
Bounce (Game), 171
Bouquet of Yarn, 56-57
Bow and Arrow, 89-90
  indoor, 119-120
Boxes, Gift Match, 65-66
Bracelet of Yarn, 129-131
Brother, Presents for, 62-63
Brownie Costume, 232-234
Bud Vase, 60
Bunny Rabbit Hat, 13

C

Cakes
  heart-shaped, 8
  round (drum), 26-27
Camphor
  fun with, 134-135
  motor made with, 129
Can Openers
  jewel trimmed, 25
  mink trimmed, 25
Can You Read These Words?
    (Game), 199
Canapés, 8
Candle, Christmas, 42-45
Candy Kisses, 74
Car Games, 176-181
Card Trick, 186
Cards, Drawing Lots With,
    169
Carpentry, 209-224
Cat, Drawing, 113
Centerpiece, May Pole, 18-19
Children's Blocks, 214-215
Children's Parade, 244-245
Christmas, 40-72
  angel, 45-47
  appliquéed apron, 143
  candles, 42-45
  decorations, 51-60
    apron, 54-55
    ball of greens, 51-52
    fans, 55-56
    flowers for coat lapel,
      57-58
    mobile, 52-53
    small wreath, 52
    table, 42

  yarn bouquet, 56-57
  golden bird's nest, 48
  greeting cards, 157-159,
    160, 162-163
  mantelpiece, 47
  presents, 54-55, 60-72
    apron, 54-55
    bud vase, 60
    dolls, 60-61
    fancy paper napkins,
      23-24
    glass paper weight, 61
    glasses case, 70
    hobby horse, 66-68
    to make, 60-68
    match boxes, 65-66
    match holders, 61-62
    neckties, 62-63
    to sew, 68-72
    shoe bag, 68-69
    table mat case, 71-72
  stocking, 70-71
  tree
    balls, 47-48
    bead star for, 50-51
    lantern, 49-50
    tarlatan, 40-41
Circus Mobile, 123-125
Circus Party, 72-74
  games, 73-74
  invitation, 72
  refreshments, 74
Clam Shell Pictures, 101-102
Clam Shell Placecards, 103
Clap a Tune (Game), 178
Cloth
  appliqué, 142-143

costumes, safety measures, 37

Clouds in Weather Forecasting, 249

Clown, Paper, 127-129

Clown White, 229

Coat Lapel, Flowers for, 57-58

Collage Contest, 184-185

Come As You Are Party, 82

Community Singing, 96

Consequences (Game), 182-183

Contests, 93-94
  collage, 184-185
  jack o'lantern, 34-35
  spool, 185

Corsage, 15

Corsage Box, 16

Costumes
  brownie, 232-234
  for the children's parade, 244-245
  fireproofing, 37
  gypsy, 237-238
  for holiday parades and parties, 228-245
  Indian hat, 242-244
  make-up, 229
  nurse, 230-232
  party, 82-83
  Pilgrim cape and bonnet for Thanksgiving, 240-242
  pirate, 236-237
  safety measures, 36-37
  scarecrow, 238
  space man, 234-236
  tramp, 237

Count the Questions (Game), 178-179

Counter for the Kitchen, 216-218

Counting Out, 88-89

Country Scene, 98

Crepe Hair, 229

Cucumber Boat, 103

Cut and Fit (Game), 201

Cutting Board, 213-214

D

Dad, Presents for, 24-25, 62-63

Decorations
  animal crackers for, 74
  balloon party, 76
  Christmas, 51-60
    apron, 54-55
    ball of greens, 51-52
    doorstop doll, 58-60
    flowers for coat lapel, 57-58
    jars, 55-56
    mobile, 52-53
    small wreath, 52
    yarn bouquet, 56-57
  for May Day party, 18-20
  Mother Goose party, 78-79
  sea shells, 99-101
  for a summer dinner party, 102-103
  treasure hunt party, 80-81

Democrat Lapel Clips, 28-29

Desk Letter Rack, 220-222

Dew in Weather Forecasting, 249

Dice, Drawing Lots With, 169

Dinah Doorstop Doll, 58-60
Dinner Parties, Decorations
    for, 102-103
Dolls
    bedspread for, 132-134
    book mark, 139-140
    doorstop, 58-60
    making, 60-61
    scarf for, 131-132
Donkey Lapel Clips, 28-29
Door Stop Doll, 58-60
Door Stop, Rock, 102
Drawing, 113-115
Drawing Lots, 169-170
Drinks, Glass for Tall, 24-25
Drum Cake, 26-27

E

Earrings, 141-142
Easter, 13-16
    bunny rabbit hat, 13
    corsage, 15, 16
    corsage box, 16
    egg tree, 13-15
    greeting cards, 157, 161
Egg Tree, 13-15
Election Day Lapel Clips,
    27-29
    for the donkey, 28-29
    for the elephant, 27-28
Elephant Lapel Clips, 27-28
England, Halloween in, 36
Envelopes, Animals Made
    From, 125-126
Eye-Brow Pencil, 229

F

Fancy Paper Napkins, 23-24

Fans for Christmas, 55-56
Father's Day Presents, 24-25
    glass for tall drinks, 24-25
    jewel trimmed beverage
      opener, 25
    mink trimmed can opener,
      25
Favors
    for May Day party, 18-20
    for Thanksgiving, 37-40
Feeding Station for Birds,
    219-220
Felt Appliqué, 142-143
Field Day, 96
Find the Cake (Game), 202
Find The Heart (Game), 8
Find the Road That Leads to
    the Runaway Horse
    (Game), 203
Finger Paint, Making,
    117-118
Firecracker Cup, 26
Flip the Cards (Game), 171
Flowers
    for the coat lapel, 57-58
    gum drop, 19
    scrambled (Game), 197
    in a 3-D picture, 126-127
Folded Tree Greeting Card,
    162-163
Forfeits, 170-171
Fourth of July
    children's parade costume,
      244-245
    refreshments, 26-27
Friends, Sick, 3-6
Fringed Napkins, 140-141

Fur Appliqué, 142

G

Games, 167-205
  for all ages, 184-188
  for an auto trip, 176-181
  back-side-to party, 82
  balloon party, 75-76
  circus party, 73-74
  drawing lots, 169-170
  family, 171-176
  guessing, 185
  Halloween party, 34-36
  for a holiday picnic, 91-94
  leap frog, 91
  Mother Goose party, 77-78
  party, 181-188
  potato race, 81-82
  racing, 35-36, 75-76, 81-82, 90-93
  scavenger hunt, 96-98, 195-196
  scrub baseball, 87-89
  for the stay-in-bed, 145-147
  summer, 87-94
  treasure hunt, 80
  up-side-down party, 81-82
  Valentine Day party, 8-9
  writing, 8-9
  see also names of games
Get Well Greeting Cards, 161
Ghosts (Game), 180-181
Gifts, see Presents
Glass Paper Weight, 61
Glass for Tall Drinks, 24-25
Glasses Case, 70
Golden Bird's Nest, 48

Grandfather, presents for, 3-6, 114
Grandmother, presents for, 3-6, 56-57, 114
Grass in a 3-D Picture, 126-127
Greens for Christmas, 51-52
Greeting Cards, 154-165
  birthday, 162
  Christmas, 157-159, 160, 162-163
  cut out, 156-157
  days to send, 164
  Easter, 157, 161
  family picture, 158-159
  folded tree, 162-163
  get well, 161
  illustrated letter, 159-160
  for a new mother, 161
  with real objects, 160-161
  spray and spatter painting, 155-156
  wedding anniversary, 164-165
Guessing Game, 185
Gum, Spirit, 229
Gum Drop Flowers, 19
Gypsy Costume, 237-238

H

Hair, Crepe, 229
Halloween, 29-37
  costumes for, 238-240
  in England, 36
  masks, 31-32
  mobile, 29-30
  Nut Crack Night, 36

party games, 34-36
safety measures, 36-37
stunts, 32-34
Hand Puppet, 121-122
Hats
  bunny rabbit, 13
  Indian, 242-244
  for a paper clown, 128-129
Helmet, Space, 235-236
Hobby Horse, 66-68
Hobby Show, 96
Hostess Gifts, 54-55, 103-104
Hot Dogs, 74
Houses in a 3-D Picture,
  126-127
How Many? (Game), 193
How Many Words? (Game),
  196-197
Hula Hula Skirt, 245

I

Ice, Pass the, 35
Ice Cream, 74
Illustrated Letter, 159-160
I'm Going To Europe
  (Game), 177
I'm Going To a Place
  Beginning With
  (Game), 178
I'm Thinking of Something
  in This Car (Game),
  177-178
Indian Hat, 242-244
Invitations
  back-side-to party, 82
  balloon party, 74-75
  circus party, 72

Mother Goose party, 77
treasure hunt birthday
    party, 79-80
up-side-down party, 81

J

Jack Be Nimble (Game),
  77-78
Jack O'Lantern Contest, 34-35
Jewel Trimmed Beverage
  Opener, 25
Jokes for April Fool's Day,
  11-12
July Fourth, *see* Fourth of
  July
Jump the Ditch (Contest), 93

K

Kitchen Counter, 216-218
Kites, 106-108

L

Lantern for Christmas Tree,
  49-50
Lapel
  clips for Election Day,
    27-29
  flowers for, 57-58
  snowman ornament, 63-64
Leaf Gathering, 93-94
Leap Frog, 91
Leather Appliqué, 142
Letter Rack, 220-222
Letters, Illustrated, 159-160
Life Pictures, 114-115
Life Size Picture, 114

Loom for Weaving, 135-136
  to wind, 136

M

Mad Hatter Party, 83
Magic Star Trick, 187
Magic Tricks, 185-187
Make-up, Costume, 229
Mantelpiece for Christmas, 47
Masks, Halloween, 31-32
Match Boxes, 65-66
Match Holders, 61-62
Mats, Weaving, 136-137
May Day, 16-20
  baskets, 16-18
  party favors and
    decorations, 18-20
Mink Trimmed Can Opener, 25
Mirror Writing, 118
Mrs. Brown Does Her
  Errands (Game), 204-205
Mobiles
  Christmas, 52-53
  circus, 123-125
  Halloween, 29-30
  for Valentine Day party, 7-8
Modelling Clay, Making, 117
Moon in Weather
  Forecasting, 250
Mother Goose Party, 77-79
  decorations, 78-79
  games, 77-78
  invitation, 77
Mother's Day Presents, 20-24

  fancy paper napkins, 23-24
  oilcloth table mats, 22-23
  straw pocket book, 20-22
Motors, Making, 129
Murder (Game), 183-184

N

Names (Game), 178, 182
Napkins
  fancy paper, 23-24
  small fringed, 140-141
Neckties, 62-63
Newspaper, Summer, 95-96
Nose Putty, 229
Number, Thinking of
  (Game), 147-151
Nurse's Uniform (Costume), 230-232
Nut Crack Night, 36
Nuts, 26

O

Obstacle Race, 92
Oilcloth Table Mats, 22-23

P

Pantomines, 172
Paper Clip Designs, 119
Paper Clown, 127-129
Paper Costumes, Safety
  Measures, 36
Paper Napkins, Fancy, 23-24
Paper Weight, 61
  rock, 102
Papier-Mache, 118
Parades, costumes for, 228-245

Parties
  apron for, 54-55
  back-side-to, 82
  balloon, 74-76
  birthday treasure hunt,
      79-81
  circus, 72-74
  come as you are, 82
  costume, 82-83, 228-245
  games, 181-188
  Halloween, 34-36
  mad hatter, 83
  Mother Goose, 77-79
  sandwich markers for,
      103-104
  ship wreck, 83
  space travel, 83
  up-side-down, 81-82
  Valentine Day, 6-9
Pass the Ice, 35
Paste, Making, 117
Peanuts, 74
Pennies, Drawing Lots
    With, 169
Pet Show, 96
Picnics
  forecasting weather for,
      249-251
  games for, 91-94
  poison ivy, 93-94
Pilgrim Cape and Bonnet for
    Thanksgiving, 240-242
Pin Cushions, 4-6
Pin the Mouse on the Clock
    (Game), 77
Pine Cone Match Holders,
    61-62

Pirate Costume, 236-237
Pistol, Spool, 120-121
Place Cards
  clam shell, 103
  Thanksgiving, 37-40
  Valentine Day party, 7
Pocket Book, Straw, 20-22
Poison Ivy, 93-94
Poker, Car, 180
Pop Corn, 74
Pot Pourri, 105
Potato Race, 81-82
Presents
  for aunts, 3-6, 56-57
  birthdays, 23-24
  blotters, 3-4
  book marks, 3
  for brother, 62
  Christmas, 23-24, 54-55,
      60-72
  for dad, 24-25, 62-63
  fancy paper napkins, 23-24
  for grandfather, 3-6, 114
  for grandmother, 3-6,
      56-57, 114
  hostess, 54-55, 103-104
  for mother, 20-24
  oilcloth table mats, 22-23
  pin cushions, 4-6
  sandwich markers, 103-104
  for sick friends, 3-6
  straw pocket book, 20-22
  Valentine's Day, 3-6
  yarn bouquet, 56-57
Puppet, Hand, 121-122
Putty, 229
Puzzles, 145, 192-205

R

Races
  back to back, 92
  balloon, 75-76
  bean, 35-36
  indoor or outdoor, 90
  obstacle, 92-93
  potato, 81-82
  sack, 90-91
  three leg, 91
  wheelbarrow, 92
Rainbows in Weather
      Forecasting, 250
Raised Cutting Board,
      213-214
Raisin Turkeys, 37-38
Recipes, 117-118
Refreshments
  back-side-to party, 82
  circus party, 74
  Fourth of July, 26-27
  up-side-down party, 82
  Valentine Day party, 8
Republican Lapel Clips, 27-28
Rhyme the Name
      (Game), 198
Ring Toss (Game), 171
Rock Door Stop, 102
Rock Paper Weight, 102
Round Cake (Drum), 26-27

S

Sack Race, 90-91
Safety Measures for
      Halloween, 36-37
Salad, Tomato Aspic, 8

Sandbox on Wheels, 222-225
Sandwich Markers, 103-104
Sandwiches, 8
Scarecrow Costume, 238
Scarfs
  for a doll, 131-132
  from hand woven
      material, 138
Scavenger Hunt, 96-98, 195-196
Scrambles, 194
  animal fair, 195
  flowers, 197
Scrap Bag Pictures, 119
Scrub Baseball, 87-89
Scrub One, 169
Sea Shells, 99-101
Sea Shore Activities, 99-102
Ship Wreck Party, 83
Shoe Bag, 68-69
Shoe Shine Stool, 209-213
Sick Friends, Valentine
      Presents for, 3-6
Silver Dust Spray, 229
Skirts
  appliquéed, 143
  hula hula, 245
Sky in Weather
      Forecasting, 249
Snapshot Greeting Cards,
      158-159
Snowman, Drawing, 113
Snowman Lapel Ornament,
      63-64
Sounds in Weather
      Forecasting, 250
Space Man Costume, 234-236
Space Travel Party, 83

Spatter Painting Greeting
    Cards, 155-156
Spirit Gum, 229
Spool Contest, 185
Spool Pistol, 120-121
Spraying Greeting Cards,
    155-156
Square Dances, 96
Stamping a Design, 144-145
Star for Christmas Trees,
    50-51
Stay-in-Bed Games, 145-147
Stencil, Making, 122-123
Sticks, Drawing Lots With,
    169
Still Sticks (Game), 94
Stocking for Christmas, 70-71
Storms in Weather
    Forecasting, 251
Straw Pocket Book, 20-22
Straws, Drawing Lots With,
    169-170
String Pictures, 118-119
Stunts, 188
    for Halloween, 32-34
Sugar Lump House, 115-116
Summer Activities
    bow and arrow, 89-90
    in the country, 98
    games, 87-94
    kites, 106-108
    parties, 102-104
    pot pourri, 105
    scavenger hunt, 96-98
    at the sea shore, 99-102
    things to take on vacation,
        108-109

    for the whole family, 96
    writing a newspaper, 95-96
Sun in Weather
    Forecasting, 250
Superstitions about the
        Weather, 255-257

T

Table Decorations
    Christmas, 42
    Mother Goose party, 78-79
    Valentine Day party, 7
Table Mat
    case, 71-72
    from hand woven material,
        138
    oilcloth, 22-23
Tarlatan Christmas Tree,
    40-41
Tell a Story (Game), 172
Thanksgiving, 37-40
    costume for, 240-242
    raisin turkeys, 37-38
    turkey place cards, 38-40
Thinking of a Number
    (Game), 147-151
3-D Picture, 126-127
Three Leg Race, 91
Tomato Aspic Salad, 8
Tommy Tucker Sing
    (Game), 78
Toss the Hearts (Game), 9
Tramp Costume, 237
Travelling Shoe Bag, 68-69
Treasure Hunt Birthday
        Party, 79-81
    decorations, 80-81

invitation, 79-80
Trees
   Christmas
      balls, 47-48
      bead star for, 50-51
      lantern, 49-50
      tarlatan, 40-41
      in a 3-D picture, 126-127
      in weather forecasting,
         250
Tricks
   for April Fool's Day, 9-11
   magic, 185-187
Turkey Place Card, 38-40

U

Up-Side-Down Party, 81-82
   games, 81-82
   invitations, 81
   refreshments, 82

V

Vacations
   forecasting weather for,
      249-251
   things to take with you,
      108-109
Valentine's Day, 3-9
   party, 6-9
   games, 8-9
   invitations, 6
   mobile, 7-8
   place cards, 7
   refreshments, 8
   table decorations, 7
   presents for, 3-6

Vanishing Penny Trick,
   185-186
Vase, Making, 60

W

Weather
   changes in, 252-254
   old sayings about, 254-255
   superstitions, 255-257
Weather Chart, 251-252
Weather Forecasting, 247-257
   chart for, 251-252
   signs to look for, 249-251
Weaving, 136-138
   loom for, 135-136
Wedding Anniversary Cards,
   164-165
What Letter Is It? (Game),
   199-200
Wheelbarrow Race, 92
Who Am I? (Game), 181-182
Wind in Weather
   Forecasting, 249-250
Witch Costume for
   Halloween, 238-240
Wreath for Christmas, 52
Writing
   backward, 118
   games, 8-9
   mirror, 118
   a newspaper, 95-96

Y

"Yap" (Game), 172-173
Yarn Bouquet, 56-57
Yarn Bracelet, 129-131